Teaching Matters

General Editors: Sydney Hill and Colin Reid

English in the Middle Years

Eric Hadley,
Senior Lecturer in English and Professional Studies
South Glamorgan Institute of Higher Education

Edward Arnold

First published in Great Britain 1985
by Edward Arnold (Publishers) Ltd,
41 Bedford Square, London WC1B 3DQ

Edward Arnold (Australia) Pty Ltd,
80 Waverley Road, Caulfield East,
Victoria 3145, Australia.

British Cataloguing in Publication Data

Hadley, Eric
   English in the middle years.
   –(Teaching matters)
   1. English language–Study and teaching Elementary
   2. English Literature–Study and teaching (Elementary)
   1. Title   II. Series
   420′.7′1242   B1576

ISBN 0 7131 09718

W 28278 [4.95 . 10.85

Acknowledgements

The author and publishers would like to thank the following for permission to
reproduce copyright material:

Mirror Group Newspapers for 'My Thoughts' by Sarah Gristwood from the
1968 Daily Mirror Children's Literary Competition and Penguin Books Ltd for
'A Boy's Head' by Miroslav Holub from Miroslav Holub: *Selected Poems*, trans.
Ian Milner and George Theiner (Penguin Modern European Poets 1967) ©
Miroslav Holub 1967, translation copyright © Penguin Books Ltd 1967.

Text set in 10/11 Baskerville
by The Word Factory Limited, Rossendale, Lancashire.
Printed and bound by Whitstable Litho.

General Editors' Preface

The books in this series provide information and advice on a wide range of educational issues for teachers who are busy, yet who are concerned to keep abreast of new developments.

The aim is practicality: slim volumes that are sources of authoritative help and swift reference, written and edited by people whose expertise in their field is backed up by experience of the everyday realities of school and classroom. The books are planned to cover well-defined topics relevant to schools in widely differing situations: subject teaching, curriculum development, areas of responsibility within schools, and the relationship of the school to the community. They are published at a time when there is a growing call for increased professional accountability in our primary and secondary schools. The 'in-service between covers' that characterizes these handbooks is designed to contribute to the vitality and development of schools and of the individuals within them.

Not only is Eric Hadley's vision of English for the 9 to 13s compelling and original, but it is also one that can be put into practice by non-specialist and specialist alike. In persuading us against 'a deadening reliance on commercially produced materials', he does not leave us searching for a substitute, but with clarity and fervour argues an approach to what happens in the lessons labelled 'English' that is firmly rooted in the passions and preoccupations of both teacher and taught, and in their collaboration as learners. He fires timely salvos at narrowness and rigidity, but not without suggesting alternatives.

In a very real sense, the most important resources for an English that is vital are in ourselves, the teachers and pupils. Eric Hadley demonstrates convincingly how with imagination these reserves of idea, idiosyncrasy, energy and involvement can best be blended with literature and other tangibles to form the basis of true learning and enrichment of a kind that teachers of English are uniquely placed to help bring about.

To all my pupils in Bristol, Suffolk and Cardiff

Contents

Introduction

In a discussion paper, the Inspectorate assert that 'with some admirable exceptions, the level of English teaching currently encountered in primary and middle schools suggests that many class teachers need greater knowledge of the subject than their initial or post-initial training has enabled them to acquire' (**1**).

That view is confirmed by my own recent observations and those of the students I train. Where expertise is lacking, there is a deadening reliance on commercially produced materials of the 'exercise' variety, which keep pupils busy, interspersed with injunctions to write a story or poem, rounded off with the desultory reading of a story or a novel.

I know that things can be better than that, and my aim in writing this book is to help all students, probationers and experienced teachers who find themselves teaching English to pupils in the 9–13 age group. Many of those teachers will be 'non-specialists', and from my primary students I know that there is often a sense of inferiority when they compare themselves with their 'specialist' secondary contemporaries. So perhaps it needs to be asserted from the start that to be a successful class teacher at primary or middle school level demands great intelligence, considerable personal resources, variety of approach, organisational skill . . . to name but a few of the qualities.

Nor will these qualities be enhanced by the administration of a package of 'greater knowledge of the subject'. I do not propose to transmit a series of ready-made lessons and resources in this book. Rather I hope to advance an argument which will provoke my teacher-readers to thought — thought about the aims of their teaching and the principles which underlie them. The reaction I intend to provoke is well summed up by a teacher recently attending one of my in-service courses who, after some weeks, came up to me and said: 'I see what you're getting at now. You're not just talking about a series of ideas or lessons — you're talking about a philosophy of English teaching'.

That puts it both too grandly and too narrowly. The more this book has advanced, the less I've found myself concerned with 'English' as it is narrowly conceived both at this level and (even more so) at the upper secondary level. Instead I've found myself turning to a consideration (albeit from the perspective of an English teacher) of how teachers and their pupils learn (or don't) through the medium of their language.

As for a 'philosophy' — all I have to depend upon is my own experience gathered over the last fifteen years of working with pupils of this age group, together with the privilege of having worked with some of those admirable 'exceptions' referred to by the Inspectorate. This book is an attempt to articulate that experience in the belief that, as teachers, we improve not as a result of exhortations, but by sharing the experience of those skilled practitioners who in their teaching are still learning themselves.

So I will not begin with dogmas dependent on the weight of my 'greater knowledge', but with some active reflections based upon my experience. These reflections do not precede the teaching I shall be describing in the rest of the book and which I hope will demonstrate their validity.

I take it as given that there is no learning without *pleasure* (both for pupils and teachers) and that what we are aiming to provide for pupils in school is a pleasurable experience. I hold with Wordsworth that: "We have no sympathy but what is propagated by pleasure; I would not be misunderstood, but whenever we sympathize with pain it will be found that this sympathy is produced and carried on by subtle combinations with .pleasure. We have no knowledge, that is, no general principles drawn from the contemplation of particular facts, but what has been built up by pleasure and exists in us by pleasure alone" (**2**).

This is not the same as saying that we aim to provide a diet of cheery fun, because we recognize that care, scrupulousness, painstakingness, delight in the finished product are pleasurable activities which may involve failure and demand the energy to start again and do better next time. It is from Marjorie Hourd, I think, that I have derived the formulation that 'Children not only want to do. They want to do their very best'.

So *pleasure* in no way excludes *seriousness*. Indeed, I might redefine my aim, and say that in my English classroom I intend to provide an environment for children in which they can be serious about themselves, their world and their books.

My experience tells me that these are the years in which children are particularly open to and full of appetite for all kinds of knowledge and experience. To know this you only have to listen to the energy with which they recount their own experience, or watch a group of children when they are taken out of school. This suggests not only that there is knowledge here for us to validate in the classroom, but also a responsibility to sustain and fulfil aspirations which are real no matter how dimly they may be perceived. I won't dwell at the moment on how so often those aspirations are defeated as children pass over the 'shadow line' dividing their primary and secondary school experience.

I would wish to place an emphasis on the *playful* aspects of learning —the way in which children reconstruct and order their world through *play*—which includes games, jokes, anecdotes, dramatization and storytelling. And, if 'play' offends, let me gloss it by asserting that it is the spirit of enquiry and speculation in the child, that sense of 'I wonder what would happen if . . .' which unites him or her to the world of the creative artist.

I recognize too that these are the years in which the child is becoming more conscious of its own experience and that it is my responsibility as a teacher to find ways in which that consciousness can articulate itself. I am trying here to recover some significance for that toary progressivist cliché that as teachers we have 'to start where the child is'. I do hold to the view that the distinctiveness of English in the curriculum derives from its being the place where the everyday knowledge and language of the child is taken most seriously. But our respect for the child's experience involves us in something more than simply confirming that experience in the name of relevance. That seems to me a conception lacking in dynamism, whereas learning is a matter of 'active construction' between teacher and pupil —neither a matter of simple transmission or dwelling in childish incoherence. Instead of talking about a 'child-centred' approach, perhaps it would be more fruitful to talk about a 'problem-centred' approach— whether it is a problem of meaning, of sympathy or of design.

Certainly, I believe that children, like adults, display intelligence according to the attitude which they display in their solution of problems. With John Holt, I hold to the view that 'intelligence is an attitude towards life and experience. The unintelligent person is the one who when faced by a problem concentrates on him/herself and not the problem' (**3**). I shall have more to say about what gets mistaken for ability and intelligence in school, how revealing and fruitful the 'mistakes' are that children make, and how attentive as teachers we need to be to the process of learning in our pupils.

I want to emphasise *variety* of experience in reading, writing, talking and listening. But I shall want to lay a particular stress on English as an *expressive art* linked with the other expressive arts areas in the curriculum —Art, Music, Movement and Drama. Therefore, I am announcing a particular interest in children as performers, writers, illustrators, adapters . . . and thinkers.

This is not an arbitrary linking on my part: it springs from my observation that children of this age find it congenial to explore and make meaning *actively* and *expressively*. Not that I wish to suggest that they are incapable of analysis or forming conceptions. The relationship between thought, feeling and expression is complex, and I hope to make some contribution to its discussion, if only by trying to recover some value for the debased currency of terms like 'creativity' and 'response', which usually thinly disguise the crudest manipulation of thought and feeling on the 'stimulus-response' model, without consideration for their formulation or articulation.

I shall be arguing, for example, that if teachers stopped for a moment to consider what it involves to be a writer, they might cease labelling the inconsequential meanderings which fill so many exercise books as 'creative'.

If I am not interested in a mode of writing which seems to me to have as its main aim pleasing the teacher, I *am* deeply interested in the nature of the relationship which develops when pupils and teacher learn together. What I particularly have in mind is that tradition of feeling which grows out of a common experience of reading, thought and discussion. I once wrote that the teacher's most significant role is to be the arbiter of the 'conversation of the classroom' (**4**). In what follows I hope to demonstrate that 'arbiter' now feels too remote.

It will be by developing the thoughts that I have just outlined that I shall come at the following issues.

1) Continuity

I shall be deliberately dealing with examples of work in English which take place over a period of time because no account of English teaching should fail to consider questions of continuity and development. My point is, however, that any account of continuity which fails to take into consideration the tradition of feeling I mentioned earlier is hopelessly barren. This is why the problems that students and probationers face are so instructive. Their planning and their attempts to establish continuity—to turn their intentions into their pupils' learning—are always *predictive*. The planning of experienced practitioners is *historical* —the experienced teacher looks back upon and synthesizes a variety of shared experiences and can presume, to a greater or lesser extent, a reciprocity of interest and feeling on the part of the pupils.

2) Assessment

Readers looking for mark-schemes or graded objectives won't find much help in the following pages. In fact, assessment is inseparable from the notion of continuity I've sketched out above. To begin with, that means the most rigorous self-assessment on the part of the teacher —of what you had in mind, and of what realised itself in the process of teaching. In other words, 'what did *you* learn?' has to be as basic a question as 'what did *they* learn?'.

3) Organization

By implication, I've already laid an emphasis on collaboration and, though I shall be looking at the successes and problems of individual children, I have a particular interest in the collective intelligence of a group or a class as something which sustains and promotes learning in the individual. Groups can clearly perform a variety of functions— activity groups, performance groups, conversation groups, and so on. They only perform no function when they are used to stream the class internally and to provide opportunities for aimless chatter while the pupils get on with their work cards.

4) Development

I have no coherent theory of development to offer. Indeed the certainty with which some teachers will prescribe what *all* children should know at, say, the age of eleven never ceases to amaze me. Even judgements about 'appropriateness' of material for certain age groups are always being exploded by day-to-day practice as are all other 'normative' judgements.

We would do better examining (and changing) the aspects of our teaching which create fear, inhibit expression, routinize intelligence and mechanize feeling. There is a great deal to ponder in Tolstoy's remark:'. . . the child lives, every side of his being strives to develop, one side overtaking another, and generally we assume that the very fact that these sides of his being are advancing is an objective and we promote mere development and not harmony of development . . .' (**5**).

5) Integration

My final aim will be to persuade teachers in primary and middle schools to use to the full the one great advantage they have over their colleagues in secondary schools. The Inspectorate touch on it in the discussion paper I began with when they say: 'Most teachers in the schools are 'general practitioners'— class teachers who are responsible for teaching all or most of the curriculum of their pupils.' (**6**) What is not then established is the liberating flexibility in the use of time this can give. The English teacher at secondary level is (or ought to be) constantly frustrated by the way continuity, motivation, a sense of achievement, the possibility of working on a large and leisurely scale are sacrificed to a fragmented timetable. 'It would be nice but I'm not sure if we've got the time today'—the result is loss of intensity and underachievement on the part of pupils and teachers alike.

The attempts of most secondary schools to overcome the problem of time by 'integrating' have usually missed the point of where 'integration', if it is to mean anything, must take place. It certainly does not lie in grandiose schemes of 'interdisciplinary organisation' which remain as external to the child as the individual 'subjects' and usually amount to the simple transmission of the lowest common denominator of 'knowledge' in the 'subjects' which have been integrated together with a massive increase in bureaucracy intent on administering the 'teaching team' and the worksheet mass-production line.

The integration I shall be speaking of is something which takes place collaboratively in the minds of pupils and their teacher, and how this can best be achieved by the 'general practitioner' and the 'specialist' is what I now propose to attend to.

1

Where shall I start?

In this chapter I investigate what we mean when we speak—particularly as beginner teachers—of 'planning our lessons' and 'preparation'. What, for example, has planning got to do with the person and personality of the teacher? I then go on to consider two examples of teaching, and explore how they represent a move away from the 'stimulus-response' pattern into a way of organizing teaching which engages both us and our pupils more actively in learning and response to each other.

Where shall I start?

Most of this book is going to deal with what I *now* think English teaching is about. But the fact that I have any idea at all, that I can even contemplate writing a book, presupposes a varied and long-term experience which I have attempted to clarify through thought, discussion and writing.

This, I have to remind myself, was not always the case. There was a time when I had no teaching past, and as for my teaching future, it was so ill-defined that it filled me with little apprehension. Nearly twenty years ago there was an eighteen-year-old who walked into a secondary modern classroom with nothing more than the newspaper he had picked up in the staffroom and thought he was going to teach thirty-five second formers . . . English.

I make my opening in this way because I want to be of assistance to those of my readers who are beginning their careers. At the same time I want to suggest the kind of effort needed from teacher trainers and experienced teachers if they are to meet the needs of those who are making a start in the profession.

Nothing is so daunting to the inexperienced as the experience of those who most want to help them. At the same time nothing can be more misleading than the way in which that experience finds its expression. The problem is that the retailing of that experience is always retrospective. What was tentative and uncertain—a moment-by-moment matter—sounds schematized and planned, coherent and assured. The more eloquent and confident the experienced teacher becomes—the more inclined to talk about 'sure fire winners' and lessons that 'can't fail'—the more on their guard the beginners should be. So, be warned!

Part of the effort I mentioned earlier lies in recognizing the gap which separates me from the beginner. I cannot now contemplate teaching a group of children without constructing an imaginary scenario in which I select from, modify and reconstruct out of countless past experiences. Equally, every piece of advice I give about materials, approaches, likely response is embedded in those experiences. Yet what beginners lack is precisely that teaching past which they need if they are to think constructively about that unknown teaching future.

Mercifully, one has to start somewhere and it is no use pretending that there could ever be some ideal 'fresh start' in which you and the pupils sprang into existence the moment the teaching started. All teaching careers begin *in media res*—they are the history of individual lives launching themselves into an involvement with the lives of others.

Yet the way in which student and beginner teachers are often encouraged to plan their first encounters with children seems to presuppose that ideal state of teaching. I would like my students to be better prepared than the ingenuous youth who walked into the classroom with a newspaper, but I don't believe that preparation means a rigid adherence to formulaic schemas involving the prodigious use of filepaper with 'enabling objectives' underlined in red. I tell my own students that I used to plan my lessons as I walked for my lift into school in the morning, and while I sat grim-faced and silent in the back of the car. I don't tell this anecdote in a cavalier spirit, rather I use it to insist that the kind of planning I have in mind is not just a routine, and that irritatingly it is not available on demand.

One of the greatest ironies in teacher training is the insistence upon detailed and clearly stated methodology at the very time when the students are most uncertain of the grounds upon which these schemes are constructed. And yet at no other time in their career will they be asked to give such a coherent account of their activities. When students encounter the ill-considered 'getting by' that so often passes for preparation in the schools to which they are attached, one can only be surprised at their lack of outrage at the hyprocisy of the demands that are being made upon them.

Worse still, they are being deflected from identifying where their real problems lie and making any creative use of that identification. It is at the beginning when one is most uncertain, and yet that very uncertainty is the best guarantee of genuine speculation and thought and openness to the experiences which the classroom will offer.

I can best demonstrate that uncertainty is not the same as unpreparedness by an analogy which ought to interest any English teacher. The analogy is between the processes involved in planning one's teaching and those involved in writing. Beside me as I write I have a synopsis of this chapter—my 'lesson-plan—aims, objectives, structure, content, all sectionalized and sub-sectionalized neatly. It 'came' very quickly and I remember completing it with a great sense of knowing what I was going to write. But wherever the 'real' chapter lies, it is not there in that synopsis, which has not even acted as a stimulus or aide-memoire. The 'real' planning is taking place every time I lift the pen from the paper and pause—usually for a long time. It has been going on consciously and unconsciously for days, submerged by thought and activity with which it is not directly connected. This attempting to articulate and give shape to a conception seems to me not at all dissimilar to the background thinking which is going on as the teacher anticipates a lesson to be taught. You may have prepared material, thought about activities and organization and speculated about various forms the lesson might take. You may have imagined several directions it might move in, just as two drafts precede this one, but the final shape will not (cannot) yield itself up. For, as with writing, the final resolution, the clarification of what it is you really wanted to do or say only takes place in the act itself.

Now, however, we need to make an important distinction between writing and teaching. As I write, I am assisted by my sense of prospective audience, but the act itself is solitary. The clarification of intention I spoke of in teaching depends upon the active participation of the pupils.

The 'clear-cut' lesson plans I castigated earlier appeal very strongly (and understandably) to students and teachers who ache for security and certainty in their dealings with children. To that frame of mind it sounds like vagueness if I advocate considered 'unpreparedness' as the approach they should adopt. Although I understand the frame of mind, I do not condone it. The problem at the beginning is that the reciprocity —the mutual clarification of intention—has largely to be taken on trust. It remains to be seen whether it will confirm itself in the relationship between teacher and pupils which can only develop over a period of time.

But, to put it simply, no planning, however 'tight' it may be, ever removed risk and uncertainty. Indeed, little worthwhile teaching takes place where no risk is involved—if the conception has achieved its expression before you walk into the classroom, what room is there for the pupils to participate and learn?

I hope it will not now seem perverse if I argue that the uncertainty which is so characteristic of beginner teachers can be conceived of as a strength rather than a weakness. Those responsible for training should be encouraging them to tolerate uncertainty instead of offering what seem to be 'answers'. For, as with children, the capacity to tolerate uncertainty is a mark of intelligence.

I have already tried to hint at a 'dynamic' notion of preparation, as a process which cannot be separated from the clarification of intention going on in the *person* doing the preparing. We need just such a dynamic, personal view when we are thinking about 'resources'. Recently, I wandered into a colleague's room after a 'resources' session. The room was full of teaching materials: charts, booklets, work cards, photocopies of documentary evidence. It was like walking into a museum—a museum of human endeavour (they were history materials) but also of teaching endeavour. No matter how 'good' the materials were, they could only exist in any dynamic sense through the transforming engagement made by the minds of teachers and their pupils.

So we need to expand our notion of 'resources' to include the personal resources of teachers and pupils, otherwise, our notion of teaching in the longer term will be bankrupt. The collection and packaging of materials does not constitute preparation, but once the habit of mind is established it is extremely difficult to break. Under the pressures of a full-time job, the enthusiastic search and collection cannot be sustained, and the tendency is to rely more and more on ready-made materials, i.e. text-books, course-books and resource boxes. Hence the respect too only for what will 'work', and the narrow pragmatism of what is meant by 'ideas'. 'This is a poor course', one young teacher remarked to me once, 'we aren't being given enough ideas'. So 'material' and 'ideas' have become synonomous, and all sense of development which must include personal development has ceased, or rather is replaced by keeping busy. In one of the first pieces I ever wrote on English teaching, I inveighed against the 'beaver mentality' which seemed to me to dominate so many classrooms with their incessant stress on 'keeping busy'. (**1**) These are the classrooms of busy, confident teachers (no 'uncertainty' now)—collecting material, laminating work cards, administering the reading lab. file, marking interminably —*anything* rather than think.

Of course, I do not deny materials to my students, but I want them to be quite clear about the status of the 'knowledge' which I try to impart. Every time I suggest an approach, a story or a poem they might try, they have to recognize that it comes embedded in the personal stake I have in that material. What I have to reconstruct for them is the history of the kind of mutual clarification of intention I spoke of earlier. Wordsworth has a marvellous definition of the kind of 'knowledge' I am trying to define. He says that the teacher should be 'rich in that knowledge which cannot exist without a liveliness of memory, preserving for him an unbroken image of the winding, excursive, and often retrograde course, along which his own intellect has passed'. (**2**)

Once 'knowledge' is defined in these terms it ought to become clear that the challenge for teacher and pupil alike is 'to determine what we are in ourselves positively' (Wordsworth again). In other words, our major concern is with the mutual development of 'self-consciousness'. This is why I have argued so far so determinedly against mechanical and managerial notions of planning and organization. Indeed I can think of no worthwhile account of one's development as a teacher that would not constitute a personal history. This is what I had in mind when I spoke earlier of the necessary 'personal stake' a teacher has in the 'material'. In this respect, James' reflections refer to teacher and pupil alike: 'no education avails for the intelligence that doesn't stir in it some *subjective* passion'. (**3**) The remarks that James then goes on to make ought to stir a salutary humility in anyone contemplating teaching—a challenge to the seductive view that if we could just get all the conditions, material resources and method 'right', learning would take place consecutively and automatically. '*Almost anything* that does so act is largely educative, *however small a figure* the process might make in a scheme of training'.

So my aim may be the development of self-consciousness, but I would be foolish in proposing the possibility of an unbroken development. The only certainty I can have, as with the progress of my lessons, is of a development 'winding, excursive and often retrograde'.

It may be argued that my emphasis so far on personal uncertainty, considered unpreparedness and speculative humility, will not encourage the self-confidence that any teacher, but particularly the beginner teacher, needs when facing the pupils. As I have already suggested, the retreat into and establishment of routines does not guarantee the kind of confidence I have in mind. Indeed, I would say that it is my responsibility to undermine false confidence, which is why after stepping inside a hygienically 'ordered' classroom, I sometimes ask my students when they are going to start *teaching* their pupils, instead of, literally and figuratively, posting lessons under the door of the classroom and withdrawing to a safe distance. Confidence is not derived from the mastery of routines, but has its roots in the person, in that 'subjective passion' I spoke of earlier. There should be humility, certainly, but at the same time you have to feel that it matters that *you* are there in that classroom. In other words, each teacher has to find for him or herself some personal vision, however incoherent to begin with, that sustains their presence in the classroom. The routines cannot motivate you, any more than they can motivate your pupils. At the beginning one has to act in a spirit of hope and optimism (else what, in the present educational climate, would you be doing in a classroom in the first place?)

The idealism and optimism of students and probationers is a familiar butt for the wit of case-hardened professionals, but as with their uncertainty and insecurity, they call for encouragement rather than dismissal. That vision will derive from many different factors—different in each individual. In some it will be the conviction derived from the effect a particularly talented teacher has had upon their lives; the conviction (hard to maintain sometimes) that education does make a difference. In others it will be no more complicated than the sense that what they enjoy they want to share with others. With others it will be bound up with notions of equity and justice; a sense that the education they themselves have received has separated them from and depended upon the exploitation of their own generation. Negatively, but nonetheless powerfully, some will be sustained by the sense that, whatever else, they will *not* teach as they themselves were taught. Others again will have sensed a connection between the arts which they themselves practise—as, for example, writers or performers—and the art they need to develop and make accessible inside the classroom.

'Character calls forth character' (I think Goethe said that) and we might gloss this by saying that only the teacher of conviction is likely to call forth conviction in his or her pupils. This in turn reminds me of an episode that the Russian writer Konstantin Paustovsky recounts which will help me to summarize this part of my argument. Paustovsky recounts how his geography teacher Cherpunov kept a collection of bottles of water in the classroom and how the bottles were labelled Rhine, Thames, Michigan, Dead Sea, Nile, Amazon and Limpopo. The boys were fascinated by the names and the stories which Cherpunov told about them—including how he himself had gathered the water from the Nile. It inspires Paustovsky to start his own collecting and the memory of Cherpunov stays with him.

However, this is not just a little anecdote about the progressive use of visual aids. Years later, Paustovsky's psychology teacher continues the story of Cherpunov:

'. . .I can tell you now that there was never anything in his bottles except ordinary water from the tap. You'll ask me why he lied to you. He rightly believed that he was stimulating your imagination . . . It was imagination, he said, that had created art, it expanded the boundaries of the world and of the mind, and communicated the quality we call poetry to our lives'. (**4**)

It is the best example I can think of to demonstrate how the quality of a teacher's vision affects the intelligence of his teaching so that it can touch and transform the intelligence and vision of his pupils.

One of the things which distinguishes the experienced practitioner from the beginner teacher is the development over a period of time of a repertoire of 'openings' which the experienced teacher falls back on in order to make a start with a new group of pupils. Many of them have become traditional but there is something in them, however simple, from which the beginner teacher can learn. There can be few of us who have not, as pupils meeting a new teacher for the first time in September, been asked to write about 'What I did in the summer holidays' or 'My first day in the new school'.

The intentions behind such injunctions to write were straightforward enough. They gave the teacher a chance to gauge quite quickly the interests and abilities of the pupils. It was a chance to see them 'at work' while providing the leisure for the teacher to observe the 'temperament' of individuals and the whole class. There was a sound instinct, I feel sure, in calling very directly upon the pupils' own experience. Equally, there was a shrewd avoidance of any long-term commitment on the part of the teacher—a wise refusal to risk starting any long-term project.

As a young teacher I rather spurned these time-hallowed conventions, determined as I was to have no truck with such shallow expediency. My refusal to 'wait and see' without recognizing that this was what my pupils were going to do, may have led me, in the case of at least one second year, to abandoning the four novels I started to read to them in the first fortnight. It may also account for the fact that at Christmas it was still the name of their previous teacher which decorated the front of their books and not mine. Pupils have to be convinced that they can take this new teacher seriously. This is why student teachers in particular have to recognize that they inherit not only a class, but also the amalgam of routines and habits that the previous teacher will have established and which define pupil expectations.

In the light of these remarks we might now lay out some general guidelines which might govern our actions and choice of materials in the opening encounters with pupils:

a) Be alert to what you can find out about them.

b) Be aware that your pupils are making judgements and discoveries about you from the start.

c) What you ask for should give some indication of what 'English' is going to involve with you.

d) Make your appeal to the experience and thoughts of your pupils—what they bring into the classroom with them.

e) Don't commit yourself too far or try to do too much—this is the first lesson and you have a whole year ahead of you.

I spoke earlier of teachers developing a repertoire of 'openings'. What I would like to do now is to dig into my own repertoire in order to try and show how my own thinking has developed and, particularly, how, in the light of experience, my own sense of what I am about in the classroom has changed. The material which I am choosing should be well known to most experienced English teachers and is easily available in anthologies. In this sense my choice is deliberate as I know that most beginner teachers have recourse to what is readily available.

So let us begin with two pieces. The first is a poem by the Czech poet, Miroslav Holub:

A Boy's Head

In it there is a space-ship
and a project
for doing away with piano lessons.
And there is
Noah's ark,
which shall be first.
And there is
an entirely new bird,
an entirely new hare,
an entirely new bumble-bee.
There is a river
that flows upwards.

There is a multiplication table.
There is anti-matter.
And it just cannot be trimmed.
I believe
that only what cannot be trimmed
is a head.
There is much promise
in the circumstance
that so many people have heads.

Miroslav Holub
(Trans. I. Milner and G. Theiner)

The second is a piece by a junior school pupil which I first found in Geoffrey Summerfield's collection *Junior Voices* (Book 1);

My Thoughts

I sometimes wonder what my mind is like inside, often I fancy that it is like this. I feel as if my mind goes round and round and round like the earth, and if my lessons make me think hard it begins to spin. In my other class it was getting all stodgy and still and lumpy and rusty. I feel as if there is a ball in my mind and it is divided into pieces—each piece stands for a different mood. This ball turns every now and then and that's what makes me change moods. I have my learning mood, my good looks mood, my happy mood, my loose end mood and my grumpy mood, my miserable mood, my thoughtful mood and my planning mood. At the moment I am writing this I am in my thoughtful mood. When I am in my thoughtful mood I think out my maths and plan stories and poems. When my kitten is in her thoughtful mood she thinks shall I pounce or not, and shall I go to sleep or not. This sort of thing goes on in my mind too. It is very hard for me to put my thoughts into words.

Sarah Gristwood Age 7.

What I need to explain now is why I chose these two particular pieces. I have already explained that I'm pondering the 'unknown' of a new class and I have tried to admit honestly the uncertainty and incoherence of the 'new' teacher. What primarily appealed to me about these two pieces was not the *purposes* to which I might put them in the classroom, but the clarification they offered of the *intentions* which might lie behind and inform these purposes. Sarah Gristwood's remark that 'It is very hard for me to put my thoughts into words' seemed to me exactly my problem, and one that I was likely to share in common with most of my potential pupils. Miroslav Holub's assertion:

'There is much promise
In the circumstances
that so many people have heads'

alerted me to the important recognition that for all my thinking about a
'class' of pupils, that class consisted of individuals all bringing with
them their own unique thoughts and experience.

There was the beginning too of an understanding on my part that in
taking other 'voices' into the English classroom, we are offering an
invitation to our pupils. An invitation to recognize in this case an
experience which we hold in common—'so many people have heads'
while, at the same time, there is an invitation to speculate about and
express what differentiates us from others, that which 'just cannot be
trimmed'.

I make so much of this because I want to delineate as clearly as I can
the kind of 'background thinking' which is essential to 'planning' and
'preparation'. The Bullock Report rightly castigates teaching which is
'determined largely by impulse' and 'directionless drift'. On the other
hand, we have to recognize that for the beginner teacher those impulses
and intentions are an essential starting point. Where can they start
other than by examining their own needs and interests and by trying to
detect the ground that connects them with the needs and interests of
their pupils—which I take Bullock to mean when it speaks of a 'studied
response to the interests of the class'. (**5**)

It was precisely the opportunity for just such a 'studied response'
which I hoped my material would provide for me.

I say provide *for me* because I think like most beginner teachers I had
a naive and touching belief in the power of my material to elicit a
response, and a very ill-defined sense of what my role might be. Indeed
the pattern of my lessons and those of many young teachers might be
represented in the following way;

1) Read it.
2) Talk about it.
3) Write about it.

This is the familiar 'stimulus-response' pattern of a great deal of
English teaching—many teachers never grow beyond it. Its seductive
appeal to beginner teachers is understandable enough because it allows
the teacher to play safe in the two areas where they are probably least
confident—namely, engaging with the class in a conversational manner
(that difficult business of 'thinking aloud') and getting the class as
individuals to engage with the material. The greatest fear is the fear of
'losing control'. So the determination is to avoid interaction at all
costs—interaction between teacher and individual pupils and (even
more risky) interaction amongst pupils. The lesson therefore moves
uneasily between two poles: public and instructional on the part of the

teacher (the address is to the group and rarely to individuals); private and solitary on the part of the pupil. The rush to the written task usually expresses an early recognition of its function as a means of control —atomizing rather than activating the class.

However, it is not my intention to dismiss and criticize, but to try and inspire confidence. And the growth of confidence implies, at least, that we recognize what we are doing even if, at the moment, there is not very much we can do about it. Even within the restricted pattern that I've presented, there are important areas where the beginner's competence is being tested and can be developed. We might, at least, ensure that we read well aloud and recognize that we are involved not simply in an act of transmission, but that in 'giving voice' to our material we offer the first act of interpretatioin for our pupils. In attending to us 'making sense' of the material, they gain their first clue to the 'sense' it may hold for them.

We might consider the clarity and helpfulness of the instructions we give, especially if, as so often happens, the material we are presenting is to act as a model for the pupils own writing. Would it help to point out that the central part of Holub's poem is a list, and that it might help them literally to 'collect their own thoughts' by listing them to begin with? Or to point out that Sarah Gristwood's piece feels very much like an extract from a diary? To do so would be to recognize that in giving instructions we have not ceased to attempt to negotiate meaning with the pupil for the sake of examining.

And, if the pupils have settled down to write, might not this be just the point to risk a little engagement and to talk to individuals rather than remaining like a sentinel at your desk or patrolling the rows like a weary policeman?

Nor would I wish to disparage the power of the material to speak for itself, however fumbling or inconsequential the teacher's mediation may be, which is why knowing what to choose is at least as important to begin with as knowing how to present. You can detect something of that power in the following pieces written by third-year junior pupils during a lesson following very much the pattern I have been describing. The only additional element was the presence of a third poem, Carl Sandburg's poem *Wilderness*, which begins; 'There is a wolf in me . . . fangs pointed for tearing gashes . . . a red tongue for raw meat . . .'

The instruction, after we had read and discussed the pieces, was to choose one of them and use that as a starting point to write about yourself and your thoughts.

Inside My Head

My mind is like a globe
Spinning round and round
Going different places,
Doing different things.

My mind is like a horse
Running free and wild
About to do anything
That comes into my mind.
I often think of television
Westerns all the time
I think about my family
A lot.
I think about
Our lessons,
Which I do not like.
I think about other people
Whoevers in my mind.

                                        Cameron

My Thoughts

I think my head is going to split open and a blaze of fire is going
to pour out. I feel that I'll go up to my bedroom and creep into
my cuddle warm bed and go to sleep. My brother annoys me
sometimes when I am in a bad mood. When I am in a good mood
I feel like teasing my brother and I feel like pulling his hair and
by then I feel hungry.

                                        Debbie

Sometimes inside my head I want to know whats happening in
the world. And in school I always want to give my teacher the
right answers. But at work the sums are hard. But at home I
always think my favourite programme is on. At bedtime I always
think what's for breakfast. At school bullies always make fun of
me and I always think they will stay nasty.

                                        Vincent

There is a dog in me a big dog that wants to have a fight and win
it and make the other one bleed to death and die . . . There's a
rabbit in me that wants to hop around play with its friends . . .
There's a big bird that flies around mountains by the sea and
swoops down to the sea and catches fish to eat . . . There's a pig
in me that scoffs his dinner down and runs around wildly and
then goes to sleep . . . There's a fish in me that swims around in
the sea and goes in underwater caves and explores the sea . . .

There's a wood in me with lots of fierce animals and that's the kind of person I am.

Dominic

Perhaps the most important point to make now is that, at last, you and your pupils really have made a start. Instead of vague imaginings and apprehensions, you have vividly and insistently demanding your attention, the intentions of your pupils. You have made the invitation, and it has been accepted. What may have begun as 'impulse', now has a chance of turning itself into a 'studied response to the interests of the class'—a response which has to include not only the writers of these pieces and their like but also the pupils who you discover were unable to or afraid to accept your invitation (like the pupil in this class who painstakingly copied out the Sarah Gristwood piece).

That studied response is bound to include questions like 'where do I go from here?' or 'how can I best help this particular pupil?' What I want to go on to suggest is that real thought about the future can now include, indeed demands as a constituent element, the question 'how else might it have gone?' In making that suggestion I am also conscious of two more spectres which haunted me as a young teacher. First, there was the fear of 'running out' in the lesson and I hope it will not have escaped notice that the opening lesson I have just been discussing uses three pieces of material. I commonly observe students seeking safety in numbers and racing through material in this way. Second, there was a longer term concern that eventually I would simply run out of ideas.

Both of these fears represent a difficulty in recognizing the need for a change of emphasis in the teacher's thinking, which is demanded by writing of the sort I have quoted above. Necessarily, as I have tried to show, the teacher's thinking at the very beginning is one-sided, but now that thinking presents itself at work in and upon the thinking of the pupils. Continuity and development of thought depends, therefore, no longer solely on the teacher's thought. So the emphasis should shift away from collecting and dreaming up, to a concentration on how the thinking which has been embarked upon can be sustained, and how a larger number of pupils can become active participants in that thinking.

It is the consideration of how that more active participation might be attained which brings me back to my earlier question—'how else might it have gone?' I actively encourage my own students to repeat lessons they have taught with other classes—modifying their approach in the light of previous experience and their growing sense of the different needs of various classes. Some of them seem to think this is cheating, whereas it seems to me a short cut to that development of a 'repertoire' I mentioned earlier, and which seems to me the experienced teacher's most valuable asset.

Let us then imagine another scenario in which the Holub poem is again our starting point, but with some important modifications. This time the pupils have the poem, but without the title being given, and initially with the last six lines missing. There is no attempt this time at class discussion or questioning. Instead, the class are asked to go back to the poem, discuss it in pairs or small groups, and then offer suggestions for a title.

These may seem like small modifications, but I think they are significant in the following ways:

1) The responsibility for thinking is shifted very quickly onto the pupils and, just as important, the teacher is diverted from that inherent tendency to stand and 'tell'.

2) The pupils have been set a 'problem' (something to which I shall return), and in returning to the text they have to pose their own questions rather than following the teacher's line of questioning. Here we might want to make a distinction between the fruitful 'guessing' they will need to do, and that other guessing of what is already in the teacher's head which dominates so many classrooms.

3) The initial instruction encourages them to tackle the detail of the poem while asking them at the same time to give some account of the whole poem. Again this is very different from the line of teacher questioning—'What does 'anti-matter' mean in line 14?' which discourages the development of understanding through an intelligent sense of the whole context.

4) Although the pupils are very quickly 'working upon' the poem, the teacher is also providing time for it to work upon them, for words and phrases to take hold and lodge.

I have tried this approach with fourth-year junior and first-year secondary pupils and found it very useful in sharpening my own sense of the way children of this age tackle a text. Part of the inadequacy of the first approach I discussed is the extent to which it takes for granted that the pupils will understand. Some of them will and, as the written work I have quoted shows, wth extraordinary maturity of insight. But one needs to be able to attend to the ideas which are only partly formed—the acuteness and the cul-de-sacs in children's thinking.

You can ascertain something of that range in these titles a fourth-year junior class proposed—Life . . . Creation . . . The Mind . . . Imagination . . . Toybox . . . Toyroom . . . Spacerocket . . . Unlike the situation with the written response, you have the chance in discussion to encourage pupils both to develop and to justify their account, and to intervene while ideas are in the process of formation. I had always presumed that most of my pupils, 'Star Wars' freaks and Black-hole buffs as many of them are, would not find too many problems with 'anti-matter'. In fact, for at least one of the boys in this group, 'matter' only made any sense in the question 'What's the matter?' 'A matter' was what he read, and 'What's a matter?' was what he heard when in discussion the question was asked 'What's anti-matter?' On the other hand, my revelation, after discussion, of the poem's actual title, *A Boy's Head*, brought the immediate retort from one girl 'Why is it a *boy's* head and not a girl's?'

That questions of this kind which have the power to demand a new direction of thought will arise is not something which can be pre-determined by the teacher. Even had one thought of it in advance, from the teacher it would never emerge with such force. All one can do is to promote the conditions under which such questions could be possible, but no question I raised 'mattered' as much as this one. It is a truism that no teacher can ask a child's questions.

However, the teacher can do something which children of this age find difficult to do for themselves—again something which did not immediately occur to me as a young teacher. As I write this, I cannot help thinking about the class of ten-year-olds I am teaching at the moment. They like listening to the stories I tell and read to them—they are appreciative listeners, quick to grasp the point without my need to labour it. Their response—oral and written—is ungrudging and often inventive. At the moment, I'm new to them and they to me, and there is an insufficiently large body of common experience for either of us to call upon. But the disconnectedness I sense needs more than time to cure it. Their regular teacher speaks of their lack of cohesiveness as a group, but I feel that the lack of cohesiveness has less to do with divergent and conflicting personalities than with lack of cohesiveness in their learning.

Just as children of this age devalue their own experience, and deny in some cases that they have any, they equally devalue their own intelligence. So intelligence in the classroom often manifests itself as a maddeningly temporary affair—immediate, like the girl's remark I quoted earlier, but rarely with a thought for development or offered half-jokingly as if the last thing one wanted to be accused of was being serious.

I shall have occasion later to try and account for this phenomenon in more detail. At this point, I simply wish to emphasize the role of the teacher as the person who encourages connection. I have already suggested that the notion of 'teacher as stimulant' is inadequate, but my attempt at encouraging my reader beyond that 'stimulus-response' model will be equally inadequate if I don't suggest a new role as 'summarizer'. Actively engage your pupils by all means, but your teaching begins at the point at which you attempt to show them how to discriminate amongst the thoughts they have, and how these thoughts might cohere.

It was partly to this purpose that in the lesson I was describing earlier I deliberately delayed introducing the last six lines of the Holub poem. For in them a new reflective note is struck, and it coincides with the note of reflection and the attempt at synthesis which I believe should characterize our teaching.

These thoughts bring me almost full circle to where I began this chapter, for they are certainly not the thoughts of a beginner teacher. Their stress on our principal aim as the growth of consciousness in our pupils reflects a very different consciousness of my own role from the one I began with. How I can justify this claim remains to be seen in the rest of this book.

However, I would like to conclude this chapter with an account of a piece of teaching which in itself may help to pull together the examples I've given and the arguments I've made. Now I have tried to show where I started, I also ought to show my reader where I have arrived.

The lesson I shall describe took the whole of one afternoon. The fourth-year junior class I was teaching had acted as 'guinea pigs' for my students, so I knew them, but it was the first time I had taken the class on my own. I was full of apprehension—the nerves that never go away. More positively I am united to that nervous young teacher by a conviction that I should demonstrate to my pupils that they can think and that I might have a part in helping them to do so. What perhaps characterizes a difference in approach is a willingness on my part nowadays to make that appeal more directly and explicitly. So, to go back to the Holub lesson briefly, I now tend to prepare my classes by doing the obvious thing—getting them to close their eyes, clear their minds and then to try *not* to think. Readers of Tolstoy will remember the young Tolstoy, at his brother Nicholas' instigation, trying desperately and without success, to go into a corner and not think of a white bear.(6) What this represents on the teacher's part is a willingness to rely more on what I call the 'anecdotal'—the little story or demonstration which draws upon the everyday world which we share with our pupils and which establishes with non-discursive economy the point of our teaching.

So today I begin by walking in and briskly handing out a piece of blank paper to each pupil ('What's this for, sir?' 'Is it a test, sir?' I haven't taught them anything yet, but still there is that Pavlovian response that somewhere there is something that could be tested.)

The paper distributed, I walk out again immediately, telling them over my shoulder that when I come back I shall ask them if they notice anything different about me. I have been in the room about a minute. It takes another minute to change glasses, scarf and carrier bag. I have hardly got over the threshold before all is revealed in a chorus of responses—even down to the detailing of the picture and lettering on the original carrier. So we have begun looking and noticing—where else might we go with this?

I empty my pockets and put it to the class—how much could they deduce about me from these contents, had I, for example, collapsed on the way into the room. There is change, old shopping lists, credit cards, library tickets, train tickets, book tokens, etc. In about twenty minutes we (they) develop a refined profile: where I live, where I lived, what station I travel in from, where I work(ed), what I eat, and so on. There is great enthusiasm as the picture begins to grow. As the pupils are finally gathering together all the pieces, one girl puts up her hand and says: 'You must be a very honest man'. For a moment I'm nonplussed and miss her point. She goes on 'You must be honest because you showed us everything you had in your pockets'.

I mention this because I have spoken of how in these first encounters children are making judgements about you. I was pleased with how things were going because I could see the confidence of the class growing as they moved from success to success. My mind I must say was not upon that other kind of confidence—confidence in you as an individual—upon which so much of our teaching depends. Perhaps, it is worth emphasizing, with the beginner teacher again in mind, that I have never seen one of those lesson flow charts with a space called 'establishing a relationship', and yet every invitation to respond carries for the child that question 'Can I trust this person? What will they do with the things I say and write?' This seems to me a better way of considering what we call relationship in learning rather than devising 'rapport-enabling-objectives'.

We had begun with problems, and the lesson continued with a new set. The class had shown that they could observe and resolve issues, so I asked them now—working together in small groups—to exercise their ingenuity on some riddles. I like riddles and the antiquity of their presence in all literatures and in the folklore of children testifies to their general appeal. They interest me too in terms of what they ask for on the part of the person attempting a solution. Painstaking accumulation—like that the class had been engaged in so far—will only take you part of the way. There has to be in addition an act of recognition, the moment when the pattern coheres and everything falls together 'in a flash', the moment when you 'see through' all the information and decide.

The riddles we looked at were taken from Michael Alexander's translation of Anglo-Saxon poetry entitled *The Earliest English Poetry* (Penguin), and there is also Kevin Crossley-Holland's translation of riddles from *The Exeter Book*.(7) So both language and syntax were demanding, as can be seen in this example; 'A miracle on the way; water became bone'.

During the time the pupils were working on the riddles there was a good deal of talk—the animatedness of that talk very different from the desultory chat of so many 'groups' I've observed. Equally, there was a good deal of toing-and-froing of group representatives checking with me to see if they were on the right lines. At one point, surreptitiously independent of the rest of his group, one boy came up to me and asked if the solution to the riddle above was 'metamorphosis'. I had a distinct feeling that 'metamorphosis' (admitting that you knew it, that is) wasn't quite 'the thing' on his table, but you'll remember what I said about trust, and how for the child it also includes finding someone who will take you seriously when you ask a serious question.

We had another delightful 'solution' to this riddle. 'Is it Jesus?' one girl asked, and as she explained I began to see how she had leapt to this solution. It starts of course with 'miracle' which she had only met in the context of Jesus, and from there to 'water became bone'—'When he walked on the water . . .'

I hope these two brief examples will explain why in our discussion of the 'answers' afterwards I so often found myself remarking, without patronage, 'well, even if that isn't the answer, it ought to be'.

We ended that afternoon with a story which I hoped would give us a chance to reflect on what we had been doing and to reflect by 'taking it in' rather than 'talking it out'. The story I read is called 'The Clever Brothers'.(8) I suggested earlier that Holub's poem had helped me to clarify my intentions in the classroom I still find literature the most suggestive resource for doing that:

'A poor man told his three sons:

'My children, we have no riches, no cattle, no land of our own. You must therefore seek fortune of another kind: learn to understand everything. Let nothing escape your notice. In place of many cattle, you will possess keen minds; instead of land, you will have quick wits. With such riches you will fare no worse than any other.'

And this is what the brothers do eventually though not without discovering, as no doubt many of my pupils that afternoon will do, that keen minds and sharp intelligence lead to suspicion and danger at the hands of the Padishahs, grand viziers and merchants who roam the world.

At all events it seemed like a good note to end on, and one that spoke to our condition that afternoon. It also allows me to suggest a fund of stories that the English teacher might draw upon and whose significance I shall return to in greater detail later.

Of course, I must not forget the written work. We had about five minutes for it at the end of the afternoon. It is rather different in character from the written work I quoted earlier and it may demonstrate the change of emphasis in my own teaching that I have been at pains to explain during the course of this chapter.

> The way the riddles and the observation jion together are because you had to think about it and use your wits to work it out and I liked working together.
>
> Michael

I quite enjoyed the work today. We had riddles and a few jokes here and there. But best of all I liked the story about the 3 wise brothers, who can tell whats in what without looking at it, or tell what a person's looking for without asking him. All my class worked very hard.

Lubna

Today we have had a good day. I think that observation and thinking is what we have been today and that I liked doing the riddles most of all although they weren't easy to do.

Jason

Mr. Hagly gave us 5 riddles. I think I liked these the best and I like the way that he explains things.

Sian

I like doing riddles because you have to work realy hard to get the answer and it is quite hard trying to get the answers. I enjoyed what we done on Friday afternoon because it was fun. After, Mr. Hadly read us a story about three brothers. That was one of the best days we had.

Sophia

The story of the three brothers, the five riddles and the talk we had at the beginning are all connected because we had to use our brains and the information we had to work things out.
This afternoon I enjoyed the story best because I like listening to storys and I enjoyed it because I liked trying to work out in my mind how the three clever brothers knew so much about the camel and the pomegranate. I found it very interesting.

Cerri

Today we had Mr. Hadley and we had a game. We had lots of fun.

Julia

2

Encouraging consciousness

This chapter has at its heart an account and analysis of a longer term piece of teaching than the single lessons discussed in the first chapter. Here two larger issues are raised about continuity of teaching and learning. How do we promote (and obstruct) learning in our pupils? What does learning look like when (and if) it happens?

2

Encouraging consciousness

I ended my first chapter with some examples of children reflecting on the activity in which they had been engaged during an English lesson. In part, my intention was to demonstrate the mixture of degrees of awareness—awareness of themselves and of their learning—in this group of children just caught on the edge of passing into the world of secondary school. I was also hoping to suggest that we encourage this awareness to develop so that they feel more in control of their own learning. I can't help feeling the vulnerability of children of this age, how ill-equipped they are to meet a school-world where, it's been argued, they *do* less and less and so many more things are *done* to them. They will certainly be vulnerable to the quick, rule-of-thumb, judgements which will be made about their 'ability'. How, for example, shall we judge this girl from the same group:

'Inside my head thoughts are made. I think of people, places, my home and family. I think of ideas, sometimes good, sometimes bad. I wonder about things. With my mind I can learn things. But what is my mind like? It is a source of information, it controls my moods, it tells me what to do and when—it gives me everything I have once seen back in detail. I also ask myself questions with my mind—then I scramble through my thoughts to bring back the answers. My thoughts—they're truly wonderful things!'

Julie

This is clearly the work of a 'very able' girl. In the best sense, it is a very self-conscious piece of writing. She wanted, she told me, to be a writer and, when I questioned the class, she turned out to be the only person who wrote regularly outside the classroom. So we'll place the "able" label on Julie, even use her as a living criterion for the kind of 'consciousness' we should be encouraging. But other thoughts occur to me—one day the whole class were working on a dramatization of a story I'd told them. Julie clearly wasn't happy: she didn't like the noise, the physical activity, the need to work with other people and the attendant arguments. She would have been happier writing and here writing is a way of avoiding getting involved. The other pupils in her group worked out a masterly solution—Julie could be narrator and she could write her part, but it had to be performed by her at the beginning of each scene. Strictly speaking, such narration was redundant, and it certainly added little to the performance.

My question is, if we call Julie 'able'—whether we then put her into an 'A' band or continue to teach her in a mixed-ability group—what are we saying? I raise this question simply to suggest that we recognize the partiality of our judgements about 'ability'. The self-consciousness which I praised in Julie earlier, like all human qualities contains within itself aspects which in changed circumstances may be 'disabling'. I am trying very hard in this passage not to over-psychologize or turn Julie into a 'case'. Julie hasn't got a 'problem'—it is simply that, like all of us, she finds certain demands upon her congenial, and others not. I am also arguing that we stop speaking of 'ability' as if it were a commodity, and recognize the various and varied 'abilities' we and our pupils display as aspects of our humanity. To begin it might help us to recognize the 'ability' which the unnamed members of Julie's group displayed in their mastery of the situation and the tact with which they handled it as an intrinsic part of their education (note *education*, not *socialization*).

I labour this point so strongly because I believe that to assert that the roots of ability and intelligence lie in the individual personality means challenging the day-to-day reality of schooling for most children. Not that there isn't an honourable and living tradition of such challenge though few have expressed it as cogently as John Holt did in his early work:

'The intelligent person, young or old, meeting a new situation or problem, opens himself up to it; he tries to take in with mind and senses everything he can about it; he thinks about *it*, instead of about himself or what it might cause to happen to him; he grapples with it boldly, imaginatively, resourcefully, and if not confidently, at least hopefully; if he fails to master it, he looks without fear or shame at his mistakes and learns what he can from them. This is intelligence. Clearly its roots lie in a certain feeling about life, and one's self with respect to life. Just so clearly, unintelligence is not what most psychologists seem to suppose, the same thing as intelligence, only less of it. It is an entirely different style of behaviour, arising out of an entirely different set of attitudes.' (**1**)

I hope that my reader will continue to bear John Holt's words in mind because a little later I shall be giving an account of a piece of teaching in which I set out very deliberately to arouse the interests of my pupils in their own learning. I wanted very much to discover to what extent a group of twelve-year-olds could make sense of the problems of learning–both for teacher and pupil.

I have to say from the start that if I thought there was a problem here, it was not apparent to most of my pupils. We may talk about these years as years of transition, years of change, but for the majority of pupils I have taught, there is no problem, at least, not in the terms I have expressed it. Indeed, they do not seem to put a consciously high value on themselves or their experience, nor are they often expected to do so. They have enthusiasms and expertise which they'll readily display or talk about. They are prone to outbursts of energy and activity, and there is little disaffection. Yet, again and again, I have a sense of pupils sleepwalking through these years. Years during which, as one middle school Head has remarked, 'having already gained a secure grasp of the basic skills of word and number, and unfettered by the imminent pressure of examinations, it should be possible to really exploit enthusiasm and curiosity'.

The best gloss I can give upon these remarks is to turn to an account I made about a year ago of a day I spent visiting a junior school:

'. . . Half the morning, a full two hours, was spent by thirty children working through English exercises—lists of words, incorrectly spelt, to be looked up in a dictionary and written down correctly—abhor, adjudicate, deceive . . . Nobody knew or cared what the words meant, many of the words were written down misspelt in a new way. What earthly purpose could be achieved by this waste of time? What thought about language had this teacher ever had? And the pupils—like their contemporaries in classroom after classroom—sleepwalk through the proceedings. They are made unconscious by it, and what they display is not enthusiasm and curiosity but patience and weary resilience . . .

. . .In the afternoon, in their dancing lesson, these sleepwalkers came to life—their energy was inexhaustible and, as I fell over my feet in the intricacies of a set, one boy kindly remarked: 'Yes, this is quite a difficult one'. And I have to include the handicapped girl who, with her legs in irons, beat out the rhythm of the dance on a tambourine. What was she thinking and feeling as she watched fifty children of her own age display what it is to have two sound legs? Who had the tact in the first place to give her the tambourine and make her comfortable? If I include this in my account then I have to try and convey the moment when a boy and girl danced down the line of the set—beautifully in step, attentive to the rhythm—and their teacher called out 'lovely'. What a moment of reciprocal pleasure—for the children, all the enjoyment of getting something right without thinking and having your mastery recognized. And the teacher—'What thought about language had he ever had?—'Lovely!' How quick and attentive of him to notice that passing, graceful moment'.

I tell that little story to establish that I want to go further than the Head I've just quoted from. Rather than talking of exploitation, I prefer to speak of celebrating the irrepressible vitality which is the only means of dissolving the deadening routine which forms its setting in school.

But how to rouse the sleepwalkers? My starting-points may seem a little surprising, and certainly they are not obviously 'relevant'—a twelfth century legend and the story of a boy and a doctor in early nineteenth century France. My references are to Kevin Crossley-Holland's retelling of a Suffolk merman legend *The Wild Man* (2) and the story of a feral child known as the Wild Boy of Aveyron. I had researched that story in Harlan Lane's book of the same name (3) in which he tells of the boy's discovery and the attempt made to 'educate' him by Jean Itard. My first encounter with the story, however, was through Francois Truffaut's powerful, if partial, film version *L'Enfant Sauvage*.

Both of these stories affected me deeply—I regard them as points of development in my own awareness about language and learning. For a long time they lay dormant, working upon me, until I could recognize a way in which the train of feelings, thoughts and problems they had set off in me might illuminate the feelings, thoughts and problems I was trying to foster in my classroom.

We began with *The Wild Man*. The text is accompanied, page for page, by Charles Keeping's illustrations, which show the merman's grace and power in his watery element and the shock of his encounter with a human world which cannot comprehend him, and out of fear binds and imprisons him. The illustrations are essential and I had each one of them put onto slide to accompany the reading.

But why start here, and not with the Wild Boy story? It seemed to me that there was essential preparatory ground to be explored. My pupils were going to be faced by the story of a boy without language, torn out of the environment in which he had survived alone and faced by a world unable to comprehend him. How do we think about someone who has no language, how do you give in language that person's thoughts? Only a story can begin to resolve that problem for us and provide the medium for our thinking. *The Wild Man* opens:

> 'Don't ask me my name. I've heard you have names. I have no name'.

Through an authorial sleight of hand which the class readily appreciated—'How can he tell the story if he can't speak?'—the Wild Man tells his own story.

So we had made a start, but I wanted the Wild Man story to lie dormant with them as it had lain for me. There would be a time to discover what seeds had taken root and how they would develop.

My more immediate problem was how to put the story of the Wild Boy in their possession. There was no version of the story to my knowledge which would have been immediately accessible to the pupils. The onus was therefore on me to tell it. In fact, I took a less direct route. News had spread slowly through France in 1798 of the discovery of an eleven- or twelve-year-old boy who had been seen looking for acorns and nuts, upon which he subsisted, and whom three sportsmen had captured. His arrival in Paris in 1799 caused a sensation and curious crowds gathered to see him. This briefly was the context I gave to the class—anything further they would have to discover by interviewing me.

So we spent an hour, the express purpose of which was for them to gather as much information as they could about the boy's state on capture, and I explained that I would base my answers on the documentary accounts that I had studied. It makes an extraordinary change as a teacher to be on the receiving end of a barrage of questions from thirty pupils. I don't need to point out the differences between this and the way children normally receive information. What it means, too, for a pupil to be a framer of questions rather than a recipient. I should add, that though I deliberately withheld nothing I only answered the questions as they were put and I resisted the temptation to lead and speculate beyond the information I had to hand.

By the end of that hour, the class had amassed in note form a considerable amount of information. What to do with it? How to give it some coherent shape? This is the point at which I always blush rather guiltily at the ease with which teachers, including myself, make apparently impossible demands on the children they teach. My suggestion was that the pupils attempt to write the boy's story up to and including his capture, and that they write it from his point of view. I did suggest that they think back to *The Wild Man*, but I also remember that all of this got rather rushed at the end of the day, and there was little time for elaboration.

Here are three extracts from the stories which they wrote:

a) I am a wild boy I dont have any body to care for and I'm very lonely. When I'm hungry I eat berrys and acorns and Nuts. When I thirsty I go down to lake and lay down on my front and put my head in it feels cool and smooth I have a lovely sence of balance when Im running. I dont feel the cold at all but when the big round thing comes up like a day like today it gives me off a patch of warmth and I love very much to sit in it When I go to sleep I sleep on a bed of moss and hay that I colected I came to be on earth like this an egg apeared from the skys and it hatched and I found by self by the shell that came from I started my life here.

b) One time when I was cracking my food hidden under a prickly bush, some creatures appeared like me but with some sort of rags on. They started to run at me but I was ready for them and ran away. They tried to catch up with me but I was too swift for them and they had gon when I looked round. As the creatures had made me a bit tired I ran on all fours and soon came to some water. I lapped some up and vanished amuong the trees to my lair. Later I opened my eyes a bright object was in the sky going down towards the forest. I was curious and ran towards it it landed in a pool and with a stick I tried to get it out. But as I shook the water the bright object shook to I was very much surprised and started to walk backwards the object rose again and was in the sky.

c) The people pushed me up onto a stone platform. I looked around me, in the big sky darkness was falling and the wind was running through my hair. Soon there was nobody about. I was glad. I could escape now. I ran to the opening, then over the soft surface and into the wood. From teere I went to the big mountains to a place where there would be no people there. When I looked to the big sky the bright round shinning thing hit my face and I felt I had to stay there. The warmth was making me smile and I forgot about the other people. But it soon disappeared and my smile had gone. The wind was going through my hair again. When I had climbed the high mountain I was very sleepy. I dropped on some fresh ground and fell asleep.

The title I gave to this chapter was *encouraging* consciousness. What these extracts display to me is something more like the teacher *forcing* consciousness. The notion of a story (with the model of *The Wild Man* behind them) seemed like a 'good idea' to me, but for most of the class that is exactly where the idea remained—inside my head. The leap into which I hurried them was simply too large, and I am even more dubious about storywriting as a means of exploration, for all that I might gloss my reasons for suggesting it by talking about 'empathy and identification'. If I had hoped that the medium of a story would 'personalize' the knowledge the pupils had culled from me, then the first two extracts suggest something more like a defeat. The 'research' and the note books are only too apparent and their 'stories' read like those BBC Schools 'dramatizations' in which each character has to get at least two 'facts' into each sentence. The third piece, on the other hand, represents a kind of triumph. It is the least 'detailed' of the pieces, because the inert facts have been replaced by the authoress' recognition of the 'true' state of the boy's feelings. Something I can clumsily point to in the subtle change indicated by and included in the repetition '. . .and the wind was running through my hair' and 'The wind was going through my hair again'—so that what began as a moment of liberation reappears as a moment of dejected realization.

I certainly don't wish to offer the third piece as a normative level of 'creativity' to which all twelve-year-olds should or could aspire. Such 'creativity' in this mode is rare—it always has been and always will be. It would be more just to the rest of the group to say that I had an interesting idea which worked for *one* person, and their difficulties faced me sharply with the dilemma of how I was going to enable rather than disable their understanding.

To start with there was an important admission to be made on my part to the group; namely, that I'd asked them to do something which had proved too difficult for the majority of them. Given our subject, this was a particularly important admission as Itard, the Wild Boy Victor's teacher, is constantly making impossible demands, getting it wrong and pushing him on—for the best of intentions.

I had by now moved on to tell them the story of Itard's attempts to 'educate' Victor—his attempts to 'socialize' him, teach him to speak and to read. There was one particularly lively discussion which emerged from Itard's discovery that despite all the 'official' medical judgements to the contrary Victor's hearing was normal:

'. . .it was remarkable that the noise occasioned by the cracking of a walnut, a fruit of which he was particularly fond, never failed to awaken his attention . . . yet this very organ betrayed an insensibility to the loudest noises, to the explosions, for instance, of fire-arms'.

I remember coming out of that lesson trying to extricate myself from a complicated explanation about stages of development and whether there was a crucial time after which developments like sight and learning would not take place. I felt stretched on such occasions and nearing the boundaries of my knowledge, but what about the children? Certainly, I think few people had ever raised such issues in such a way with them, but what sense were they making of it? What was the point of all this knowledge—did they perceive it any differently from the 'knowledge' that was retailed in their other lessons?

Here I think it may be apposite to quote from the teaching journal that I was keeping at the time:

'On Monday afternoons the third year middle school group I am working with have Humanities for the first session and English for the second. Their Humanities lessons follow a familiar pattern each week. 3S are submerged with the rest of the third year and sit uncomfortably at tables and on the floor to listen to a twenty-minute 'lead-lesson'. The Humanities 'Theme' for the term is 'Empire and Colonization'—today we are dealing with the discovery of Australia, having whisked through American colonization, the emancipation of the slaves and British colonization already. It is the fourth week of term! The teacher talks for twenty minutes, the class make notes—there is no discussion. There is usually a guide sheet (looking suspiciously like the teacher's notes) or a work sheet and for the second half of the lesson the class return to their own classroom with their own teacher, and write up their notes with the 'aid' of the guide sheet.

This afternoon one remark strikes me. The teacher describes the activities of European traders in the Spice Islands and the waters north of Australia and casually remarks that the Europeans were 'bound to bump into Australia'. The remark drops into the pool of ignorance and no one asks why, if the Europeans were 'bound to', the seafaring peoples of the East Indies who had sailed the same waters for many thousands of years hadn't 'bumped' into it? The answer to my own question relates to the inertness of the teaching I am observing, how it 'unlearns' and 'makes stupid' the children who so patiently endure it and a problem I am facing in my own teaching of 3S. Isn't the answer that you have to think something is going to be there before you find it, your expectations have to be alerted before you make the discovery—as with those Europeans who expected to discover Terra Australia?

I carry these thoughts with me through break and into my lesson with 3S. We have been working on the story of the Wild Boy of Aveyron, the feral child discovered in late eighteenth century France and upon whom an experiment in education was conducted by the pioneering educator, Itard. My reflections on the Humanities lesson and the problems 3S are having with the work focus around some remarks made by Itard about this boy. He remarks that although the child has sight, hearing, and so on, his 'vision' is non-existent, due to lack of stimulation. To what extent has 'vision' been stimulated in that lesson or by what I've been doing? Last week we were discussing the problems he had faced in trying to teach someone who has no language. They seem unable to grasp the enormity of the problem, nor was my attempt to make it real by asking them about how they feel about *their* difficulties with learning very fruitful. Just as there were no questions in the previous lesson, they seem not to sense that they have any problems—even the boy I've seen sweat with panic when I was trying to explain Base 5 to him.

Is the work too hard, are the class too stupid—Itard gave his boy hot baths and rubbed him with rough towels to stimulate him—what should I do?'

For the moment I'll withhold any comments on the teaching I've described or my own thinking at the time. Instead, I'll proceed with my account of the lesson which followed on immediately from the Humanities session:

'With me this week I have an OHP transparency, on it I've written five lines of text. I choose two pupils and seat them opposite each other, the 'teacher' holds the transparency, I instruct the 'pupil' to read the text, which is, of course, reversed from her point of view. The rest of the class I instruct to sit round and observe what happens. The pupil, a fluent reader, takes sixteen minutes to stumble and hesitate through the text. I have used this exercise before with adults and students as a 'shock tactic' to try and bring home some of the problems we underestimate in the act of reading—but never before with children. After the girl has finished, I ask the rest of the class what they observed. The first responses concentrate on the 'pupil's' obvious frustration and growing exhaustion, details like shifting in her seat, peering at the text, wiping her hand across her face, while they notice too, the teacher's immobility. And then there are two responses which make me think back to the issues raised by the Humanities lesson. One boy comments on the 'teacher', and says: 'She's supposed to be the teacher and she wants to help the girl but she doesn't know how to'. Immediately another boy chips in, and says: 'But the girl (the pupil) is no good either' and goes on to gloss this remark by saying 'She wants to be helped, but she doesn't know how to use the help she might get'. Now I think we are ready to go back and talk about the problems Itard was facing'.

I'm not going to waste my reader's time with a detailed analysis of the Humanities lesson—it isn't a question of comparing two styles of teaching or contrasting 'cognitive' and 'affective' modes of learning. The heart of the analysis we need to make is there in the phrase I use in my original account—'the pool of *ignorance*'. To call such 'teaching' Gradgrindery is to commit a sentimental error. Gradgrind was a man with a mission who believed in education and thought that 'facts' were important. We (and I mean those of us who were brought up on chapter 1 of '*Hard Times*') make a mistake if we think it is Gradgrind—a man of principle—that we have to contend with. Unprincipled vacuity is what we have to contend with—not force-feeding with knowledge, but the expropriation and elimination of knowledge by default.

The boys who commented in the way I have described in the course of my lesson seem to me to have acted with intelligence. Their remarks seem to me to be evidence of a remarkable ability to see to the heart of the problem, and to synthesize all of the issues we had raised in previous lessons. The conciseness of their expression is enviable: it clarified for me and for the rest of the group all that we'd been stumbling around and trying to articulate.

What caused this outburst of intelligence, this extraordinary break with routine? In trying to answer my own question, I don't offer the following list as a guarantee for creative thinking in the classroom, which is why at the head of my list I have to place:

1) Luck.
2) I spoke earlier of a break with routine. This was the first lesson that I, in any significant way, had broken with routine, and I mean by that something rather more than *variety* of approach. There had been plenty of variety—stories, illustrations, I'd instructed them, appealed to their personal experience, tried to get them to empathize, we'd talked about all manner of behaviour, but . . . for the first time:
   a) They had behaviour to examine.
   b) In this sense the classroom had become an area for experiment.

c) I hadn't anticipated their findings or their mode of expression. This is the hardest thing for any teacher to do no matter how committed he or she may be to children finding their own meaning. Yet it is precisely that sense of having your thought and its expression constantly anticipated (most classroom 'discussion' is dominated by it) which checks creative thinking.

3) Though I've tried to give an honest account of my own sense of inadequacy, I seem to have sustained interest, and in the lesson itself to have focused intense interest on what proved to be a promising problem.

4) That degree of intensity—'seriousness' is perhaps another word we might use—must to some extent be dependent upon imitation of and infection by the teacher. It is impossible when (as in the case of the Humanities lesson) it is absent in the teacher.

5) This in itself suggests that it is not so much difficulty of thought which excludes others from learning, as the absence of any model of thinking. As Etienne Gilson remarks 'unless he (the teacher) is actually *thinking aloud* and engaging his own intellectual activity . . . the teacher does not actually teach'.(**4**)

6) What this implies is a reciprocal relationship between teacher and pupil, for if I hope to clarify meaning in another I have to be open myself to clarification, which is why I insist that these pupils were not only engaged in an act of self-expression. They also made expression in a new way possible for all of us.

Certainly this lesson promoted a fresh sense of endeavour in all of us—both an awareness of the problems which Itard and his pupil faced, and a greater readiness to admit the problems we all faced in learning. I have already mentioned in my journal account the boy who was struggling with Base 5. His situation and mine will be familiar to anyone who has sought to help a pupil who is encountering difficulties in number work or reading—namely, the dilemma the teacher faces in recognizing that well-meant personal attention can increase the pupil's panic and fear of the problem before him. His attempt at the earlier piece of written work about the Wild Boy had not been very successful, but, when I returned to the subject of times when we had found it difficult to learn or understand something, this is what he produced:

'I was just starting school and I brought some flash card,ome —the letters were 'and', 'the', 'of'. I din't now them so I was learning with my dad. I got all hot and swetty; my dad started to shout at me. I cryed and ran up the stairs, he came after me and then hit me. My mum said, 'I will train him and learn him'. I felt much better with my mum'.

We recognize, I think, in this moving and dignified little piece, a different kind of consciousness from that which the boys managed in our 'experimental' lesson. It displays none of their 'eureka-like' grasp of a generalized truth living in the situation before us. Nor does it have the command necessary to enter powerfully into someone else's feelings that the girl demonstrated earlier in her piece about the Wild Boy. Nevertheless it seems to me the work of someone who has faced and gained power over his own experience. It is also an 'intelligent' piece of writing—you will remember Holt's words:

> 'Clearly its (i.e. intelligence's) roots lie in a certain feeling about life, and one's self with respect to life'.

As I suggested at the beginning of this chapter, 'consciousness' and 'intelligence' will manifest themselves in many different ways in any 'mixed-ability' group. But there is another kind of consciousness which for want of a term readily to hand I'll call 'group-consciousness'. The boy I have just been discussing has clearly found a way of facing and articulating his own experience in a unique and authentically personal manner. But, as I have already argued, his ability to do so has been promoted by the general sense of clarification which emerged from our earlier experimental lesson—a clarification framed in a manner very different from the one which he seems to have found congenial.

I am saying nothing more than that in recognizing individual intelligence we should have an eye in our teaching to the communal and collaborative intelligence which sustains the individual. The boy I have been discussing has also been a party to all the stories, discussions, writing, experiments we have engaged in. It seems obvious to me that the experience of a common set of reference points is essential to the development of our pupils. One only has to contrast the depressed atmosphere in 'lower stream' groups—groups in which the only common experience is failure, and where there is no other standard of intelligent behaviour on the part of your peers to live up to or live by—to understand the need. And, as I've already suggested, special help and 'remediation' can itself, however good the intention, confirm paralysis rather than empower our pupils.

It seems equally obvious to me that continuity of teaching and learning finds its location in that communal and collaborative intelligence I have just touched on. It is still true that 'so much English work still suffers from a lack of coherent purpose and continuity', and this will remain true while we emphasize the place of 'materials' and external 'structures' as the determinants of continuity. Where else does continuity lie in the piece of teaching I have been describing other than in the minds and feelings of teacher and pupils working upon what comes to be recognized as a problem shared in common?

Retrospectively, there now seems a rightness in the fact that we completed this period of intense activity with a final shared experience —sitting together in the little darkened school assembly room and watching Truffaut's *L'Enfant Sauvage*. I take that occasion as a high-water mark of the 'seriousness' this group were capable of, a measure of the expectations it was possible to have of these twelve-year-olds who had never seen a 'foreign' film, an occasion for the integration of thought and feeling which is the fullest antithesis I can offer to the disintegration of 'group consciousness' going on in the Humanities lesson I described earlier.

However, I won't end this chapter on that note—it isn't any part of my intention to make claims for what goes on in English lessons at the expense of other areas of the curriculum. Instead, I would sooner end with a Humanities lesson which bears more closely upon the analysis I have been making.

The second year (ten- and eleven-year-olds) had been considering in their Humanities lessons the development of a basic technology by man—specifically, the discovery of fire. They had been very confident about the many different techniques: creating a spark with flints, the various friction methods, focussing the heat of the sun, and so on. So, along with one of my colleagues, we spent a whole afternoon trying to make fire. We had all the materials to hand, and the pupils embarked on the experiment with great enthusiasm and tremendous confidence that they were going to succeed. When we gathered together at the end of the afternoon they were in a rather chastened mood.

The flints had worked fine, but no one had found a way of directing them onto the kindling. In fact, you couldn't even see the sparks unless you conducted the operation in a very dark place (the stock cupboard proved to be perfect). As for the friction experimenters, they brought back a tale of raw hands, charred pieces of string, worn out pieces of wood—but no ignition. As for kindling, the pupils had started off with piles of straw gathered from the neighbouring fields, but it had clearly proved incombustible by the methods they had employed, and they had had no more luck with little piles of sawdust, twigs, scraps of material, with which, as the afternoon wore on, they had replaced the straw.

In one sense, they had wasted a whole afternoon and all of their attempts had ended in failure. Yet in our discussion at the end of the day all kinds of critical questions began to emerge; making fire and keeping it was very hard, why would anybody bother to do it if it cost so much pain and effort, had anybody 'made it' in the first place, or had people depended on natural outbreaks and then made sure they kept it and carried it with them (as many nomadic groups do, of course), had the 'inventions'—flint, friction sticks, etc.—come after the 'discovery'?

I hope this little example will confirm the analysis I was attempting to make earlier, and demonstrate the kind of conditions we all —English teachers, Humanities teachers, Science teachers alike—need to promote if we are seriously interested in fostering 'creative' thinking in our pupils. You will notice certain features present from my earlier analysis:

1) The absence of 'anticipation'. For once, the pupils were allowed their head. No one said 'It won't work' or 'There's not time, so I'll tell you'.

2) There was the focus of intense interest on a 'problem', and thus a readiness to try again and again, and to sustain failure.

3) Finally, there is the explosion of the 'received idea', as new problems emerge which the conventional wisdom doesn't explain, or doesn't even seem to have taken into account.

3

Writing by accident

This is a chapter about knowledge—the kind of knowledge that children bring into the classroom with them and which they can sometimes write about. There is also an attempt to analyse in some detail the inner workings and contours of that knowledge and how it differs from the knowledge which characteristically seems to dominate schools.

3

Writing by accident

It may seem a little flippant on my part to speak of 'accident' in a book with the avowed intention of helping teachers to consider the principles which underlie their teaching and to enable their pupils to become more conscious of their own learning. The contradiction in my title may be less apparent if I ask my reader to consider again what we might learn from the change in the nature of their thinking which seems to occur when children are liberated from the sense of having their every thought anticipated by the teacher.

If we check through our experience, I believe that most of us would admit to times when we were disappointed at the response of our pupils compared with the amount of effort and energy we had put into our teaching. Equally, there will have been times where we are surprised at what our pupils have made of what seemed, on reflection, teaching which we considered lack-lustre and banal. I particularly have in mind the chastening experience of marking work done in your absence which can sometimes raise the doubt as to whether your permanent absence might be more beneficial—that your pupils learn in spite of rather than because of you.

Of course, I'm not advocating that the teacher 'do nothing', but what I hope to demonstrate is that there is a great deal to be learned from these occasions when as teachers we are 'not doing', those occasions when *our* intentions do not swamp the intentions of our pupils.

So I'll begin by looking at a piece of writing by an eleven-year-old girl which emerges very much from the kind of context I've just described. This is a piece of writing done to fill up time—the title is, in fact, taken from a writing competition current at the time. There has been very little 'preparation', and it doesn't relate as a piece of writing directly to any activities the class were engaged in.

Thursday 2nd October 1980
What happened to me in 1979.

You could see her each day running around in her cage. When I come to see her each day she would run to the wire. I used to poke my fingers through the wire and Maria my rabbit would nibble them. Each night as I lay down in bed I would think about her, every day before I

went to school I would go and see her. I could remember that once
Maria had 11 babies and they all used to look so small and pink as they
lay in there soft bed of hay and hair after a few weeks they was walking
about in the cage when I put the carrot pellings in the cage they all
used to go for them as well as Maria there mother. On July 30th 1978
the baby rabbits crawled out of the cage they was now about a month
old and they looked so small and cuddley. My mum said that I had to
sell them and I wasnt allowed to keep any of them. On July 31st I went
down to see Maria and her babies but when I counted them I found out
that there was only 10 so I went back and told my Mum. She said that
she would go down and have a look to see if I was right when I came
home from school my Mum told me that Maria had sat on the on that I
loved the most I had called him Scrog because all of his fur used to stick
up. On the same day my Mum had put an advert up in a shop window
saying "RABBITS FOR SALE 50P EACH CALL AT 7 CHESTNUT
CLOSE 6 till 8 o'clock" When all of my rabbits had been brought I was
very unhappy but still they was out of the way. Later on during the
months Maria died in September I found her frozen to death in her
cage on a Saturday morning. I knew why she died it was because she
only had a wooden hut and all of the other rabbits had cages made out
of old oil drums and thats the sad thing that happened to me in 1979.

My initial response to this piece of writing is that *whatever* the
teacher's intentions were in setting the 'subject', the child writer has
recognized that an opportunity to say something had presented itself
and has grasped it fully. Precisely because of the absence in this case of
much in the way of adult (teacher) injunctions or suggestions we get a
clear indication of what a *child* of this age might use writing for. I don't
in saying this wish to suggest that what we have before us is some kind
of natural, spontaneous outpouring—it is written and not spoken—but
I am interested in the differences between this piece and some of the
written work that children of this age group produce at the more direct
instigation of their teachers.

But to return to my initial response, and to what seems to me the
essential point: here is someone who has found a *purpose* for writing.
What the absence of teacher direction emphasizes is that finding a
purpose has to be an autonomous act. So this 'accident' paradoxically
may show us a way but it also defines the limits of what we can do for
children. In other words, it may suggest fruitful 'subjects' for us to
promote with our pupils—subjects which depend upon their personal
experience, but we cannot supply the urgent need to write them down.

I labour this point because I think we often take the merits and
purposes of writing to be self-evident to children. Only recently I had
occasion to argue with a teacher who was complaining about the
disparity between her pupils' oral and written fluency: 'If only they
would remember to write down what they say'. The recognition of a

purpose has to include an understanding that writing is a very different business from saying. Such a recognition is implicit in this piece. It may remind us in places of spoken anecdote but its 'writteness' is much more striking—from its opening uncomfortable syntax, its shifting tenses, its whole problem with 'settling' to a style.

If teachers are not often very good at promoting purposes for writing, they do expend a good deal of effort on promoting a methodology of writing. They offer models; they suggest certain kinds of vocabulary. It may be illuminating, therefore, to consider in more detail this piece of writing where the pupil has been left to her own devices.

I have suggested that this is a very 'written' piece, and that its 'writteness' involves giving a narrative shape to the personal experience. It seems to me (and I shall take up this argument again in the next chapter) that this narrative differs significantly from 'stories' as they're so often conceived in school. It contains, that is, few of the surface features and techniques which I regularly observe English teachers encouraging their pupils to adopt:

1) There is no 'description', contextual or otherwise; no use of 'good' words and so a marked absence of what we might call the 'sellotape method of composition'.

2) There is no explicit characterization, no overt psychologizing, no dialogue. The piece abounds with opportunities for all three. The main narrative has innumerable little stories embedded in it—these are left unexploited.

3) An audience is obviously presumed but there is no attempt to milk the situation and establish 'interest' or 'sympathy'. The audience is addressed directly 'You could see . . .' and events are reported to it.

In the absence of such qualities this clearly cannot be a piece of 'creative' writing, but then like all pieces of authentic writing, this piece explodes categories. If 'creative' won't do, which label shall we choose: 'informational', 'personal' . . .?

There is no interest here in 'representation', that would be a diversion:

> '. . .They do not, like parrot or ape
> Imitate just for the sake of imitation, unconcerned
> What they imitate, just to show that they
> Can imitate; no, they
> Have a point to put across'. (**1**)

All of the energy goes into 'presentation', as directly and economically as possible. You don't doubt for a moment the seriousness of the experience—she tells you: 'I would think about her . . . I was very unhappy . . . that's the sad thing that happened to me . . .' And 'the point' is inescapable: 'RABBITS FOR SALE . . . but still they was out of the way'—powerless to do anything else, you accept, even if it means accepting someone else's judgement. But here I'm already doing something this writer never does—in other words, I can't leave events to speak for themselves and I can't resist the temptation to manipulate my audience by the power of my own rhetoric. Here I'm introducing that 'adult mental mode' that Lawrence castigates so sharply. Faced by a piece of writing in which false feeling and straining for sympathetic effect is so conspicuously absent we might, at least, have the tact to recognize that 'we must not strain the *sympathies* of a child, in *any* direction, particularly the direction of love and pity . . . A child's sagacity is better than an adult understanding, anyhow'. (**2**)

If a child of eleven is capable of this degree of 'sagacity', capable of this degree of criticism of her own experience, then methodologies of writing, training in how to create 'effects' seem less important than encouraging the sense that amongst the purposes of writing criticism of experience, 'having a point to put across' is paramount. To put it another way, what I'm suggesting is that we give as much attention to the politics of writing as we do to the aesthetics of writing. This remark may take some of the smugness out of the assertion I make in my introduction that 'the distinctive place of English in the curriculum derives from it being the place where the everyday knowledge and language of the child is taken most seriously'. This isn't a powerful piece of writing *because* it's based on personal experience, but because personal meaning, knowledge and judgement hold together whereas often outside (and inside) English writing involves a disjunction between personal meaning and 'knowledge'. This child has invented a discourse in which her 'wisdom' can find expression which challenges us to expand the 'discourses' available within the context of English.

It is self-evident from the piece of writing we have just been examining that our pupils live in a personal world charged with preoccupations and meanings. To illustrate further my earlier point about the disjunction between personal meaning and 'knowledge', I'd like to go on to describe something which happened later in the year to this pupil and all her contemporaries.

As part of their work in Humanities, a visit had been arranged to an open-air agricultural museum. We arrived—all three coach loads of us—and proceeded to make our way about the exhibits: farm machinery, implements, photographs, barns, a reconstructed mill . . . we had the whole day. I am always fascinated by the behaviour of pupils and teachers on such occasions and I am still uncertain about what is the best thing to do. On the one hand, the pupils are being 'drenched in experience'. Released from the confines of school, they, as often as not, rush around madly, their eyes skim over objects, and in half an hour a couple of impromptu football matches have started, or a group has milled back to the coach wondering if it's time to break out the packed lunches. I am reminded, in fact, of what I said earlier about Itards' Wild Boy—all of these children had their faculties, but it was as if they could not 'see'. In order to 'see' it is insufficient to be bathed in 'experience', to be overwhelmed by it. You have to know what to look for, or, at least, to anticipate that there are discoveries to be made.

There had been considerable disagreement amongst us—the teachers—about how we should meet this problem. Two groups had been armed by their teachers with work sheets and they raced on ahead identifying objects, making little drawings and answering questions. Here I have to disclose a prejudice based upon my disquiet at the antics of the birdwatching fraternity, or at least that section of it known as 'tickers'. The 'tickers' I have met seem to me to have no interest whatsoever in birds, but seem to derive immense mechanical satisfaction from collecting sightings and recording them. Our 'tickers' returned back quickly from their skim around the museum declaring that they'd 'done it'. We have all experienced the doom that these words spell to any notion we might have had about development, further discussion, going back and repeating.

Two events stick out in my mind about that day, and they offer an interesting contrast to what I've so far described. In the centre of the site was a large barn which had been filled with Victorian school furniture: desks, chairs, visual aids, implements. It had, in fact, been used as the 'school-room' for the TV adaptation of Ronald Blythe's *Akenfield*. A colleague and I collected together about fifty of the pupils, sat them down in the desks and had an impromptu 'lesson' which we started in 'strict' fashion from the colossal teachers desk. We must have spent about half an hour in that gloomy barn with its hard, uncomfortable seats, the pupils packed in like sardines, some of them having to sit in the little 'baby' seats ranged in front of the teacher's desk. What can I say other than that they went out with something of the 'feel' of that school, and that they were full of the differences (and likenesses) to their own school experience.

A little later we came to a windpump—a windmill-like structure that had been used for raising water and drainage purposes. There was a good wind and we managed to persuade the curator to set it in motion. As the blades began to gather speed, quite literally, I have never seen so much excitement. First, there is that vertiginous feeling which comes from standing inside the sweep of the blade with your back against the mill sides—the rush of air and the queasy sense that you might take off at any moment. This is quickly followed by the irresistible invitation to the 'dare' of running through the gap as the blades speed by. As the pupils (and teachers) raced in and out, we had a glimpse of that world of risk and adventure which drives parents to distraction as they worry about what will happen to their offspring if they 'let them out'.

The world of 'instruction' and the world of 'experience' are always at odds in the way I've just hinted at—schools, no matter how progressively committed they are to 'first-hand experience' are still schools. The Opies made some suggestive remarks about this tension in their introduction to *Children's Games in Street and Playground* (**3**), when they spoke of the truly dangerous world children roam in their play, and the adult invented 'play-areas' and 'adventure playgrounds'. Risk and adventure lie in the world of waste ground, dilapidated buildings and rusting car wrecks precisely because they contain what adults *don't* want. 'Play-areas', however heavily disguised, demonstrate what adults want—entrances, fences, boundaries and 'play-leaders'.

The educational 'tickers' always want to overleap the child's own mode of experiencing, instead of understanding it as a condition of their learning. Thus they commit themselves again to the round of 'teacher anticipation' I spoke of in an earlier chapter and the self-fulfilling prophecies which usually accompany it.

These were the thoughts I carried away from this experience, and that I had in mind as I anticipated another visit which had been arranged to a local village and its church. My heart sank at the thought of more work sheets, 'trails', and so on, but, at the same time, I wanted the children to see and notice more, and to find a way of recording their experiences.

So we set off one morning the following week on our walk down to the village. It takes about three-quarters of an hour and involves walking through the very 'unrural' housing estate most of the pupils come from, crossing a very busy trunk road and then going across the fields to the village. We chatted fairly idly all the way about what we could see — who lived where, people's gardens, how noisy and busy the main road was, what was in the fields, stopping to 'feed' horses,—until gradually the outskirts of the village came into view.

All we had taken with us were some clipboards, plain paper and pencils, and now we made our first stop and made the first of a series of sketches. I had decided on sketching as a way of concentrating the children's attention and we made a number along the way and in the churchyard itself. More than anything else I wanted to see if we could avoid that 'eye-skimming' I mentioned earlier. I made my own sketches and walked about with the children in the churchyard as they wandered and explored the exterior of the church, the monuments and the gravestones.

Rather to my surprise we hardly had time to go inside the church itself, though we did have a brief encounter with another group who were madly milling about inside.

In the afternoon back at school we collected our sketches together and talked about what we'd seen and how we might record our visit. I told them how many people—particularly artists and poets—had kept records (words and drawings) of this kind of walk, and had often used the journals later as starting points for writing or painting, and how they'd all been people who had looked closely at the world about them. I read them an extract from Hopkins' journal where he describes a walk in early May in the countryside around Oxford:

'. . .Over the green water of the river passing the slums of the town and under its bridges swallows shooting, blue and purple above and showing their amber-tinged breasts reflected in the water, their flight unsteady with wagging wings and leaning first to one side and then the other. Peewits flying. Towards sunset the sky partly swept, as often, with moist white cloud, tailing off across which are morsels of grey-black woolly clouds. Sun seemed to make a bright liquid hole in this . . .' (**4**)

In the end I asked them to take one of their sketches and 'work it up' into a more finished picture, and alongside it to write down what they had been thinking about or feeling as they made the original sketch. Here are some examples of what they wrote:

The Tower

1) I leaned against a wall it felt cold on my back I could feel the ivy that grew on the wall.
There was a gentle breeze and the trees that hung over my head moved slightly.
An eerie feeling ran down my backbone.
The soil below my feet was very soft and I got the feeling that I was sinking rapidly but I wasn't.

2) I walked around the church until I came to a dark gloomy corner of the church it was hidden by a tall yew tree I went into the corner I felt like a streack of cold air went through me The corner seemed like a trap Their beside me was a trough full of water. There my reflection looked back at me and I saw little leaves of the yew tree in the water and near the trough was an old Rickety Rackety door I don't think it was in use eney more.

3) When I did my first skest it was of the tower Round me was lots of space and it made me fill small but the coulor of me stood out because the Church is very grim and stony.

4) When I drew a steetch of the pyramid I thought that I was on top of it and I could see the whole of the village all a round me. When I drew it I could think I would just blast off like a white tornado as well on top of the pyramid.

The grave

5) The grave out side shaped like a coffin had cracks where the slabs were joined together inside there was some Ivy Craig to have a better look pulled out a slabe further out came a musty small. you could just see the light through the other side I wouldnt have liked to be buried.

These little fragments of writing are obviously very different in form and status from the piece of writing I discussed at the beginning of the chapter. Clearly, they are less of a fruitful 'accident' than that first piece, and as I've tried to suggest in my account, there was a good deal more conscious activity on my part. Nevertheless, they are 'accidental' in that the writing went beyond anything I'd intended or expected. If my intentions were centred around close observation of and concentration on the 'objective' world, then the pupils have interpreted that intention quite differently. Indeed, the model I'd offered—the journal account by Hopkins—seems to have been the least significant influence.

I argued earlier that the lack of teacher injunction had provided an 'openness' which had been seized (filled would perhaps be more accurate) by the child writer. In these examples, something more like 'indirection' rather than lack of direction seems to have been at work. For, by having their attention focussed beyond themselves, each of the children seem to have found the room to place themselves centrally in their writing.

What they produce is markedly different from any of the 'personal' writing which I've examined so far, and where the appeal on my part has been *directly* to their experience. If they place themselves centrally in their writing, they do so by placing themselves centrally in relation to their world—a world which they feel themselves to be sharply distinctive from 'but the colour of me stood out', and yet which they are intimately related to 'Their beside me was a trough full of water. There my reflection looked back at me . . .'

It has taken me some years to find an adequate account for what I believe to be happening here, and I find the following remarks by Wordsworth helpful in clarifying my own thoughts: 'What then does the Poet? He considers man and the objects that surround him as *acting and reacting* upon each other, so as to produce an infinite complexity of pain and pleasure . . . to this knowledge which all men carry about with them, and to these sympathies in which *without any other discipline than that of our daily life* we are fitted to take delight, the Poet principally directs his attention. He considers man and nature as *essentially adapted to each other*, and the mind of man as naturally the mirror of the fairest and most interesting qualities of nature'. (5)

'Acting and reacting upon' that seems to me to be exactly the note of this writing and an 'infinite complexity of pain and pleasure'—that's there in abundance too. It's there particularly in the fourth example which represents a notable triumph for its author, certainly disciplined in his daily life by failure at school and the contempt of his peers, but who contemplates his brief moment of power over it (and them) all as he 'blasts off' from the 'pyramid' (one of the monuments in the churchyard).

As for the teacher's role, I hold to my remarks about the principle of indirection. I don't believe that direct address to these childrens' sense of themselves would have created the conditions for such a response. None of these children usually talked or wrote readily about their experience, and being directed to concentrate beyond themselves through another medium of expression (the sketching), being released from 'responding' directly was crucial in ways which surprised both me and them.

I can now expand, too, on my earlier warning about 'overleaping the child's own mode of experiencing' because we have before us now an expression of it, whereas before, in my anecdotes, I could only suggest its presence. But in speaking of the *child's* own mode of experiencing, I am aware of the danger of suggesting that we are in the presence of some kind of primitive emotional or linguistic stage which we have to go through before we achieve 'objective' maturity. Again Wordsworth is helpful: 'The knowledge both of the Poet and the Man of Science is pleasure; but the knowledge of the one cleaves to us as a necessary part of our existence, our natural and unalienable inheritance; the other is a personal and individual acquisition, slow to come to us and by no habitual and direct sympathy connecting us with our fellow beings'.

What this suggests to me is that instead of wasting our time in arguments about the 'cognitive' and 'affective' domains in education and feeling smug as English teachers about the superiority of the 'poetic' we might rather find ways of validating and developing that knowledge 'which all men carry about with them'. These ten-year-olds seem to have no problem in recognizing that they and their world act and react upon each other, and the onus is just as much upon the English teacher as the Science teacher not to force a disconnection in that sense of relatedness.

To enforce that point I need to go back to our walk: 'In the open air, out of school . . . new relations are established between pupil and teacher: freer, simpler and more truthful—those very relations which seem to us the ideal that school should aim at'. (**6**) Not my account, but Tolstoy's opening remarks to an account of a walk he took with some of the pupils from his school. My point is that the sense of relatedness I spoke of above depends upon the relations established between pupil and teacher.

The conditions for the writing we have been examining were not simply my intentions, their interpretation by the pupils, the experience even, but the way in which all these factors were shaped by what was 'between' us during that morning and afternoon. That would have to include our talk during the morning and not simply the 'subject' of our talk—the things we noticed along the way, me pointing things out—but the sense that there was time and leisure for that kind of talk to take place (how regularly do our pupils experience that either at home or at school?) There was another kind of shaping too—the distinction between the activity of the morning—the looking, exploring—and the tranquility of the afternoon, the essential opportunity to take stock and reflect. I think this writing depended on that kind of rhythm to the day—the lack of urgency and the deliberate 'possibility' of the task—its shortness.

In emphasizing the importance of the relationship between teacher and pupils, I would not be misunderstood. The teachers I described earlier who sent their pupils off to 'tick' objects, negated their relationship with their pupils, and made the discovery of relationship (and therefore meaning) impossible to them. 'Ticking' or 'summing' is a meaningless activity which disintegrates and denies the relationship between parts. If the children's writing I have been discussing speaks of anything, it speaks of the discovery of relationship, and therefore a potential for the intelligent construction of meaning. Their capacity to integrate their experience, what gives 'shape' to their writing depends upon the 'relationship in learning' which I've tried to sketch out:

'The world has its influence as nature and as society on the child. He is educated by the elements, by air and light and the life of plants and animals, and he is *educated* by *relationships*'. (**7**)

4

Children as writers

In this chapter, I look at some of the problems which children have as writers, particularly as writers of stories. The concern is with the ways in which we might help children to be more conscious of the problems involved in writing, and again, with how we sometimes defeat our pupils and our own best intentions.

4

Children as writers

I was very struck recently by a remark made by the children's writer, Jan Mark. Speaking of children as writers, she said: 'Each one of them is uniquely qualified to write about themselves . . . The first duty of a teacher is to convince them of the immense value of what they know'. (**1**) It is a remark which can act as a summary for a good deal of my argument so far.

However, the words of another great writer and teacher tally more closely with my own experience and, I suspect, that of many other English teachers. Tolstoy, writing about his own pupils' efforts at storywriting said:

'Many intelligent and talented pupils have written trivia; they would write 'the fire broke out, they began to haul, and I came out into the street', and nothing would emerge, in spite of the fact that the subject of the composition was a rich one, and the events described had left a deep impression on the child . . . I tried many different approaches . . . it did not work'. (**2**)

In this chapter, I want to consider further some of the obstacles that stand in the way of children writing—some of their own making; some the result of teacher activity.

Here is the beginning of a story written by Dean, who is eleven. He wrote it one weekend and gave it to me on Monday morning:

The Three Tasks of Clayten

One day a giant Eagle called Glase was captured by a with called Grezalda who has turned Glase into her castle. But one day a capenter's son called Kalyton fell in love with the king's daughter and the next day he asked for her hand in marrage. The king agreed but he remembered that when she was a baby a witch called Grezelda cast a spell over her that would only be broken when Glace was free. "I'll do it, I'll have a bash at it" said Klayton "you must be made" said the king "no I love her and I'm going to do it" "OK we'd better get you some armor and arms then" said the king. So he was of on his adventure. The king had told him of three tasks he had to do he had to get the sheild of truth from claw mountain and the scrimitar from

Devilscreep and to call his name three times. So Clayten called his name three times and pure white pegasus with golden wings flew to him he mounted it and flew of to claw mountain . . .

I want to begin with some positive remarks about this piece. In the first place, no one asked him to write it, so he already sets himself apart from most of his contemporaries in that he now knows something of what it means to choose to write. As an autonomous writer, he'll probably have learned something of the disparity between intention and performance—the way in which that mighty epic full of event and character reveals itself in the writing as four and a half flat pages in a cheap note book. There are times too when he demonstrates that essential intoxication with words and their movement which leads to the adoption of a particular manner because you enjoy the feel of it so much: 'So Clayten called his name three times and pure white pegasus with golden wings flew to him . . .'

I don't wish to underestimate the importance of the factors I've mentioned. Clearly, Dean feels the 'need' to write. If his writing is derivative—of the books he's read, the films and TV that he's watched —then so are the beginning attempts of many writers (George Eliot's schoolgirl attempts aren't very impressive). Nevertheless, his writing seems to me to exemplify the dislocation of personal knowledge and expression, and it represents an all too familiar cul-de-sac in children's writing. For all the appearance of striking phrases, good vocabulary ('truth beamed out of the shield' he writes later), surface fluency—it is incoherent. Words have control over him rather than him controlling the word. What it lacks is 'authority', and in this sense it contrasts very sharply with the 'rabbits piece', I considered in the previous chapter. For a definition of 'authority', I'll return again to Jan Mark: 'I do myself like to know how things work. It is essential, you know, and you've got to let it show. It weakens the reader's confidence if you generalize and gloss over. You need to demand to be believed. Your knowledge gives you an authority which transmits itself to the reader.'

It strikes me in this piece that Dean, who is an argumentative and opinionated boy, full of energy and varied experience, reveals nothing of what he 'knows'. Extraordinary as it may seem, it is the capacity for 'making things up'—what gets loosely termed as 'imagination'—which English teachers and their pupils seem to value as opposed to knowledge.

Recently I was visiting a third-year junior classroom where pupils were writing stories using characters from the 'comic' ghost story their teacher had been reading. Their stories were tedious and derivative in a familiar 'fantasy' vein. Yet embedded in one boy's story I noticed the following phrases: 'Ghosts feel like the skin of a chicken', 'She feels like a squashed-up pea with broken cement mixed in a smelly toilet', 'The hag is like a old rotten bag that has been dumped in a pool of mud'.

The class weren't 'very good', the teacher told me, and particularly not very good at writing stories. It struck me that they were likely to remain not 'very good', while they were diverted into writing 'fantasy' and 'book stories', and while what they could do went unrecognized. This boy's capacity to record his 'real' environment—the acres of disused railway sidings, abandoned industrial sites and decaying housing which surround his school—is only too apparent.

Next I might recall the thirty-five 'ghost stories' I read while visiting a student. The class was a 'top-set', second-year comprehensive class full of 'intelligent and talented pupils' writing 'trivia'. I noted only one new development, but on the increase I suspect—amongst the familiar facility with churchyards, tombs, vampires and so on, a new facility: 'where the axe had entered all the sinews and muscles were exposed . . . brain tissue exploded everywhere.'

I won't dwell on these examples but they ought to demonstrate that any encouragement of story writing responsibly conceived has to include a continuing consideration of the contradictory power inherent in the fictional worlds we introduce our pupils to, and that which daily they watch and absorb. I had occasion earlier to mention the 'sagacity' of children. Part of the development of that sagacity might include encouraging a healthy disregard for certain kinds of fiction and its purveyors. '*Huckleberry Finn*' as a text may be beyond most of our pupils in this age range, but to teachers it offers an inexhaustible store of reflections upon 'fictions' and 'reality'. Fluency, literacy, and articulateness—all highly valued in school—may not be unmixed blessings. I know that Tom Sawyer is fluent and articulate, but I prefer Huck's 'sagacity', his healthy disregard for fiction, as apart from anything else it confirms my sense that fiction which denies my capacity to test it against my experience confuses rather than clarifies my sense of reality:

'Shucks, it ain't no use to talk to you, Huck Finn. You don't seem to know anything, somehow—perfect sap-head.'

I thought all this over for two or three days, and then I reckoned I would see if there was anything in it. I got an old tin lamp . . . and rubbed and rubbed . . . but it wasn't no use, none of the genies come. So then I judged that all that stuff was just one of Tom Sawyer's lies. I reckoned he believed in the A-rabs and the elephants but as for me I think different. It had all the marks of a Sunday school'. (**3**)

I'll continue with one of my own attempts at helping a class to write stories. I'd been trying to practise my own principle of encouraging my pupils to think about how stories 'work' as a background to their own attempts. We began the lesson by playing 'Chinese Whispers', and then I read to them the text of Pat Hutchins' little picture book *The Surprise Party* (**4**), where the narrative depends entirely on a message being transformed as it passes from creature to creature and then being reconstituted. I followed this—they'd all dismissively 'got the point'—by reading Jan Mark's hilarious short story about crossed purposes and mistaken messages—*Send 3/4d I'm Going to A Dance.* (**5**) It had been an enjoyable lesson in elementary structuralism for eleven-year-olds, and in the dying minutes remaining to us I asked them to write down a memory of any time they'd been at the centre of a misunderstanding.

At the beginning of our next lesson we looked at the collection of anecdotes we'd assembled. When they'd re-read their own and their friends' pieces, I asked them if they could tell me what they thought was different about what they'd written from the stories they'd read or heard read to them. And what they thought they would need to do to turn their little pieces into 'stories'.

We quickly assembled a list of differences:

1) They'd written as if you (the reader) knew the person(s) they were writing about—so they clearly understood that 'audience' affects the way you write.

2) Accordingly, they hadn't bothered to tell their audience *about* the person—what they looked like, what kind of person they were, where they lived . . .

3) Unlike 'books', they hadn't bothered much with conversation.

4) They thought, too, in a 'story' that it would probably be someone else telling the story—it wouldn't be 'I' all the time. So again, there's some indication that they understand different narrative roles and how this may affect the telling of a story.

They had no difficulty in assembling these points, and they confirm what most teachers would recognize about pupils of this age. They've assimilated—even the non-readers—a wide variety of 'models' of stories. They have quite a sophisticated sense of how they work and they know what they like. They recognized that their little pieces weren't really 'very exciting', 'not much happening in them'. 'Real' stories are about war, spies, ghosts, hi-jacking, space, horses. This genre writing or viewing they always describe, interestingly, as being more 'realistic'.

After we'd had this discussion I asked them if they would swap their piece with a friend and see if they could re-write it as a 'story'. In doing this I was trying to resolve some of the problems which seem to beset children when they embark upon writing a story:

1) I hoped I was taking away the problem of 'invention'. I wasn't asking them to be original and 'make up' a story. I hoped too that I was doing more than setting a subject or giving a beginning usually seems to achieve. Children, in my experience, don't usually have problems with getting started. More often they falter because they can't see where they're going. So they run out of steam or can't disentangle and choose from amongst the many different directions the story seems to be taking them in. I hoped that having a 'story' would give a sense of purpose and direction, but, again, conceived in a different spirit to the well-intentioned but mechanical 'planning'—plot, list of characters, and so on—which teachers often insist that their pupils perform in advance of writing.

2) I hoped that in asking them to consider someone else's 'real' story I could divert them away from genre writing, and indirectly encourage them to allow their stories to be informed by their own experience. For it is precisely their own experience which in storytelling they seem most ready to devalue—'nothing ever happens to me', 'it's boring round here'. Stories are things that (other) people 'make up', 'imagine', or 'invent', and teachers (unlike writers) seem to place a high value on 'imagination' and 'originality'.

3) These pupils like most of their contemporaries are resistant to the idea of 'redrafting'. In part, this is a reflection of the view they have of the purposes of writing and how it will be received. Most writing is a 'one-off' affair—answering questions, writing up notes, repeating in written form what the teacher or book says. They write for the teacher as examiner who 'corrects' their work. Even 'creative writing' tends to be perceived in this way, and most 'rewriting' is copying up for best or display after correction by the teacher.

It's hardly surprising that the idea of significant change and reworking should make little sense. It only begins to make sense when you have some autonomy of purpose as a writer—you have your own intentions *and* standards to satisfy—and when these are recognized and met by your audience.

In reworking someone else's story I was looking for a way of breaking this deadlock while, at the same time, providing another interested party other than the teacher for the story.

Here is Sophia's original piece and Cerri's 'reworking' of it:

'I remember when I was about 3 years old my mum left me in the room, so I went straight upstairs and started to mess about with the things. First of all I climbed on the chair a opened a tub of my mum's cream a smudged it all over the mirror, then I took all the clothes out of the cupboard and through them all over the floor. Then when I heard my mum coming up the stairs I quickly hid in the cupboard. When my mum came up, she went mad. That was realy funny.'

'One morning when Sophia woke up, she felt like being naughty so when her mother came up stairs to see if she was asleep she shut her eyes and pretended to be asleep. So her mother thought to herself oh she's asleep, I can nip down to the shop. When her mother had gone Sophia climbed out of her bed and crept into her mothers bedroom and opened a tub of hand cream then she smeared it all over the mirror. Sophia giggled to herself and when she saw what a mess she had made, it made her even more determined to be naughty so when all the jug of handcream had been smeared all over the mirror, she ran over to her mother's wardrobe. Smiling to herself she flung open the doors of the wardrobe and pulled out all the clothes and threw them on the floor. Just as she was thinking what else to do, she heard her mother coming; quickly she jumped into the wardrobe and closed the doors. Her mother came up and looked into Sophia's bedroom, Seeing that Sophia was not there, she ran into her bedroom. As soon as Sophia's mother saw the mess that her bedroom was in, her face turned from pale pink to white. She threw her arms up in despair and ran towards the wardrobe and flung open the door she picked up the frightened Sophia and carried her downstairs. She sat her on the settee and asked why she had been naughty. "I did not mean it said Sophia," and she started to cry again. "Never mind," said Sophia's mother we cant be good all the time. So Sophia's mother tied up the mess and no more was said about it.'

I shall come back to look at this transformation in more detail later. It is quite unique and no one in the rest of class managed anything like it. Much more typical is what Hayley does to Collette's original. This is Collette's relaxed, anecdotal opening:

'I was about 6 and my mother sent me on an erran to the shop she told me to get some pears, so I was saying pear's, pear's, pear's over and over in my head . . .' Her directness of treatment is sacrificed for this in Hayley's version:

'There was once a girl called Collette. Collette was six year's old. She had dark brown hair and brown eyes. Collette's mother had auburn hair and brown eyes. Collette is a very nice girl sometimes that is. When Collette isn't kind and good, Collette is very naughty. She gets on very well with her mother, that is when Collette is in a good mood . . .'

'It did not work'—however well-intentioned and carefully thought out the activity may have been on my part. Most of the class, like Hayley, took the points we had raised in discussion, and applied them as an inert set of rules to the writing they were 'reworking'. Hayley's version is more striking than most in that from time to time a personal voice emerges because she cannot resist scoring off Collette '. . .that is when Collette is in a good mood . . .' To put the point simply, just because you have some sense of 'how' stories work is no guarantee that you will be able to write them. If this were so, then all University English graduates would be novelists, poets and dramatists.

Cerri not only 'knows how' in this sense. She clearly *likes* writing stories. She confidently takes hold of Sophia's piece, grasps its potential, and reshapes it with great fluency to her own ends. She is in command of her material from the moment the first phrase emerges. That first phrase 'one morning' takes us straight into novel writing with its omniscient narrator, detailed setting, psychological interest, internalization of thought and feeling, 'slice of life' ending.

It is interesting now to look at Cerri's own original anecdote:

'One day I was on my way to school when my mother asked to post a letter. All on the way to the letter box I was going post the letter, post the letter, post the letter, and when I came to the letter box I walked right past it still saying, post the letter, post the letter. In the end I had to run back and post it and I was late for school. When I got to school I came up to class and mrs. marks had not arived so I sat down and got something out and when mrs. marks got back she did not know that I was late.'

This piece suggests to me that writing 'fiction' for Cerri has a liberating effect on her writing. Her story is much more complex, much more intelligent and more 'personal'. In her story, she's capable of comedy, (melo)drama and tenderness. It ought to alert us to the fact that the relationship between 'personal experience' and the use that can be made of it in 'fiction' is a complicated one.

Here is perhaps the point to introduce some further remarks by Tolstoy about his pupils: 'They did not understand the main point: why write? and what is good about writing down? They did not understand art—the beauty of expressing life in words and the absorbing power of that art.'

I think that Tolstoy's account captures the energy and pace of Cerri's story. Here, for different purposes to my example in the last chapter is someone who knows 'what is good about writing down'.

I don't know *how* you make that act of consciousness for someone else, or by what systematic process you can *teach* someone to write like that. The danger with all 'systems' is—as many of this class demonstrated—that you may teach the system, but what intimations of artfulness were present are dissipated. I'm pleased with Cerri's story beccause she has clearly found a form in which her intelligence and sympathies can be realized—there is something to encourage and develop there. Should we worry that the rest of her classmates don't seem to be able to manage what she does—do all of them have to become competent story writers in her vein?

I only ask these questions because so much prestige seems to have attached itself to storywriting in the context of English teaching—even when, unlike Cerri's story, the stories represent a diversion of intelligence, or denial of experience and a facility of dubious value. Cerri's story would, I think, please many English teachers because of the way it approximates to a model of 'naturalistic' fiction. It is the model which dominates English teaching at secondary level, both in terms of the storywriting which is encouraged and the fiction which teachers mediate to their pupils. I shall have more to say about 'naturalism' in later chapters, but as a form of story it represents only one amongst many.

It certainly wasn't the form that Lubna turned to in her original piece about misunderstandings:

'One morning Gupter was told by his master to buy one dozen eggs That got Gupter worried because he can not speak english, because he comes from India. So his master taught him how to say one dozen eggs. It took quite a while, but Gupter got the hang of it. So off he went along the sidewalk when suddenly . . . he saw a pretty woman on the other side waring a ra ra skirt. Gupter never saw anything like it before. As he was walking he kept on repeating one dozen materil, on and on and on finily he got to the egg shop and asked for one dozen materil this got the dealer confused, and these are the very words of the dealer, you got the wrong place mate. So poor old Gupter had to act a chicken and finally got his one dozen eggs. And went home.'

Lubna also likes writing stories: she even shares the same opening words as Cerri, though significantly Lubna's 'one morning' signals a quite different intention, and the entry into a quite different mode of storywriting. 'One morning . . .' heralds the world of scurrilous jokes and folk-tale—The History of Stupid Gupta. Here swiftly unfolding incident and disdainful narrative comment are what matter. They both work to make a point, not to reveal a psychology. That 'point', which reveals her distinctive cultural perspective, makes itself felt where the formality of her direct address to an audience meets the devastating 'realism' of the shopkeeper—'these are the very words of the dealer', "you got the wrong place mate."

Corum does not like writing stories:

'When I go home I go and get something to eat and drink and say to my mum 'can I go out she says yes I go out to play and come back about 7 o'clock wotch t.v. till 8 go in my room till 10 and then go to bed.'

Not only does he not like writing stories, his writing denies that he has any story to tell. Watching him painfully write this piece, trying to persuade him that he had got something to write as he came out time and time again to say 'I can't think of nothing', it is the solitary nature of storywriting that defeats him. Nothing exposes you like the blank page. So in the end he goes for safety and non-communication.

Throwing children like Corum back on their own resources—demanding that they be expressive and creative—seems like a waste of time to me. Nor does it seem any part of my business to cause denial of communication in someone who is by instinct sociable and communicative. For all the help and easing of the problem I thought I was providing, I haven't provided him with a problem he can work on or, more importantly, work on with others.

What we might more fruitfully be offering pupils like Corum will be the subject of my next chapter, but I would like to end with some further thoughts about pupils like Cerri, who have demonstrated by the age of eleven a talent for writing stories. Interestingly in his account of his work with his pupils, Tolstoy goes on to describe how he achieved some success only by working alongside his pupils—actively engaging with them while they were in the process of writing.

I have described a similar experiment with pupils elsewhere. (6) But working in this way does raise some problems which have to be recognized. Tolstoy ended up working with three pupils only, and he and his pupils had unlimited time within which to work intensively. These are not the day-to-day conditions under which teachers and pupils work: thirty pupils demand your attention and they write, in secondary school certainly, in bursts of about thirty minutes duration, in classrooms which discourage the privacy needed for reflection.

Perhaps the analogy we need to develop is with a subject like music—if talented performers are recognized in that area as deserving special attention in small groups so that those talents can be developed, then why should writers not receive the same recognition and help? This is the only way I can see in which the tokenism of what passes for an interest in the development of 'creativity' can be challenged. And these children need the assistance and guidance of 'experts'—*writers*, not (on the whole) English teachers: just as one wouldn't dream of entrusting instrumental tuition to non-performers.

This would involve a massive expansion of the existing 'writers in school' provision, and increased access to extra-curricular events and residential courses where children could meet and work with writers.

5

Playing with stories

This chapter begins by looking at a number of ways in which we can enable children to feel that they are more in control of stories and the experiences which they offer. This leads on to a discussion of how we can develop and encourage a critical sense in our pupils. The latter part of the chapter is devoted to children engaged in critical discussion of the texts they receive and demonstrating their capacity to argue and discriminate about them, the ways in which they are illustrated and the way in which they represent the world to which these children belong.

5

Playing with stories

I want to return now to the defeat of Corum and many of his contemporaries in the face of the self-reflective demands made by individualistic forms of storywriting and 'personal' writing. As I have remarked elsewhere, to be successful in these forms 'requires that you feel the significance of your own experience—your own distinctiveness and that of other people'. (**1**)

Reading for children like Corum often produces the same problem —again it is an isolating activity in which they are thrown back on their own resources and deprived of a sociable context. This is particularly true in those classrooms where 'reading' has become a competitive activity, and where your status depends on where you are in the hierarchy of gold cards, magenta cards, and so on. Nor do I believe that the answer to their 'problems' with reading and writing lies in 'withdrawal' and 'remediation.' *More than anyone else* they need the sustaining presence of the class and their groups of friends, and the address of a teacher who presumes that they can do things, rather than a teacher, however well-intentioned, who defines them as subjects for special treatment.

I am presuming, too, a teacher who recognizes that telling and reading stories is the single most important function they have to perform inside the classroom; that it is a central and not a peripheral activity in an avowed policy of encouraging confidence in our pupils and of enabling rather than disabling their intelligence. Crucial to that growth of confidence is a sense that in stories we can locate an area which we can play around with, exploit and change, rather than constantly feeling that we are at their mercy. So I am on the look out for stories that invite that kind of speculative approach.

Some stories announce their intention quite clearly:

'Once upon a time there were three bears, seven dwarfs, five gorillas, a frog prince, some sleeping beauties, a wolf, a dinosaur, a Mad Hatter, a steamboat, four firemen on a fire engine, a crocodile with a clock in it, a considerable number of giant beanstalks—and a little boy named Jeremiah Obadiah Jackenory Jones . . .' (**2**)

Jeremiah in the Dark Woods by Janet and Allan Ahlberg is a story which very much invites its young reader to join in the fun of recognizing how a whole host of familiar stories, formulas and characters can be transformed and reworked. I've found it a very fruitful starting point with my own pupils to convince them of just how many stories they do know, and how well they know them and how they work. This in itself involves a recognition of just how much our enjoyment in reading depends on all the other stories we know, and how large a part picking up references and allusions plays in that enjoyment.

Jeremiah in the Dark Woods is a story I 'use' as a model for encouraging pupils to experiment with and rework familiar stories. In the first place, it has the virtue of bringing to mind all those stories like *Little Red Riding Hood, Goldilocks and the Three Bears*, that are so embedded in your consciousness that you can hardly remember how or when you first got to know them (that in itself makes a fascinating area for discussion).

It is at this point that I usually introduce my pupils to *What Else Might Have Happened to Little Red Riding Hood* (**3**)—a reworking of that story in flow diagram form, which exploits alternative routes, endings, introduction of new characters, etc. When we've familiarized ourselves with the method, I ask the class to choose a story and make an attempt at a flow diagram themselves. They can work on it individually, but I find it works equally well as something accomplished in pairs or as a group.

I have a strong memory of encouraging this approach with some very sceptical teachers I was working with. One of the most sceptical did point out, however, after he had tried it with a class that *for once* his pupils who normally gave up and left their stories uncompleted had completed their diagrams. Bearing in mind my earlier caveat about 'sure fire winners', we might account for this in the following way: when writing a 'conventional' story, many children have no idea where they are going. There is no overriding 'logic' to the direction of their story, no 'map' which indicates a destination or reference points which might assist in steering a course. Here there is a sustaining logic to which one can make constant reference—the original story which is 'known'. This has a liberating effect, I believe, because it allows the child to concentrate on the logic of localized diversions without worrying too much about the general direction. It is the tension between 'what is going to happen next' and 'where is all this leading to in the end' which leads to exhaustion on the part of many young story writers.

The diagrammatic, 'short-hand' way of sketching the story out is also helpful. It enables you to check back and forth along the logic of events, try out alternatives, close off unpromising directions, bail out at cul-de-sacs. These techniques seem to me essential to a notion of successful 'planning'—at the moment I'm surrounded by a multitude of bits of paper covered in 'sketches' for this chapter linked together with lines and arrows. To return to my point about the growth of confidence, the ability to plan is essential to a sense of being in command of one's own experience.

The ability to plan is dependent on our capacity to make intelligent *predictions* and stories have an important part to play in developing that capacity. Indeed, prediction is inseparable from their enjoyment. Something brought home to me the other day by a girl's *sotto voce* commentary throughout my reading of a story: 'Oh, I know what's going to happen . . . I think I've worked it out . . . I know what kind of story this is going to be . . .'

A story I often use when I want to make prediction a class activity is the Grimm story *The Six Servants*. (**4**) It belongs to that well-worked genre of tales where a hero is faced by impossible tasks which can only be accomplished with the assistance of men or creatures with particular gifts. In this case, the young man collects on his journey: a man of voracious appetite, a tall man, a man with superhuman hearing, a man with piercing vision, a sharp sighted man, and a man of contrary nature, who freezes when it is hot, and burns when it is cold.

One's pleasure in the story lies in anticipating how and in what combinations the young man will employ his six servants to defeat the sorcerer-queen who stands between him and his princess. So this is what we do—I stop the story at each of the tasks and the class write down their 'solution.' Before we move on we check out the various solutions, discuss their merits, and appraise them in the light of what happens in the story.

It is a very simple place to start and one that I try to make as deliberately 'unsolemn' as possible. It depends obviously on stories which are strongly 'patterned' and which appeal to the admiration I find my pupils have for ingenuity, resourcefulness and sheer downright cunning.

I now want to move to an example which I hope will complicate and widen the scope of the argument. In one sense it may seem to follow on naturally from the encouragement of prediction and the exploration of alternative routes. This time the pupils (top juniors in this case) have been encouraged to write alternative endings to a story.

The story in question is another one from the Grimm repertoire —*Frau Trude* (often translated as *Mrs. Gertrude*). The text is very short: a girl 'stubborn and insolent' is warned by her parents not to visit Mrs. Gertrude who is a 'wicked woman.' The girl refuses, however, and I always stop the story at: 'but the child paid no attention . . . and went to see her all the same . . .' With the pupils I was speaking of earlier in mind I deliberately choose a short story, limited in character and incident, and I tell them that the point at which I've stopped is only a short paragraph from the end. Yet, however restricted my aims may have been, the childrens' response raises larger issues of learning and suggests a more ambitious development in the teaching:

a) . . .She was determined to go there. So when she went to bed she made a rope out of bed sheets and climbed out the window and went to the house. An old lady took her in. As soon as she steped in her face started to crinkle and her hair went grey and her nails started to go long and black. She ran to the door and screemed. As soon as she stepped out she turned into a scelloton and thats the last we saw of her.

b) The girl entered the house all sorts of frightening noises came throughout every crevice and Mrs. Girtrude came out in a black coat and bloody teeth and when the girl saw her, her hair stood on end and the lady invited her in and said, 'come in my dear' and the girl ran for miles and miles and was never seen again, but it turned out that Mrs. Girtrude had only used a dummy and a walkie talkie and she was one one of the nicest people that ever lived.

c) The girl sneaked out and gose to see Miss Germentued. She knocks on the door and the door just opens. The girl walked in and the door slams behind her. Then a voice said come in and the old lady said what brought you here. The girl said Nothink. The old lady said do you want a cup of tea the girl said yes please. Miss Germentrood got up brout her a cup of tea and the girl gulped down and suddenly she started to grow. The girl screemed and ran out back to her home and the next day her mother came in and saw a giant sized girl. Sudonly the girl woke up and saw her mother and mother said I warned you.

d) The girl goes to Mrs. Gertrude's house and she finds more out about Mrs. Gertrude and she turns out to be a very nice lady and the girl gets very fond of her and she finds out that it's all roomers the girl gets very fond of the lady and the girls friends don't talk to her she gets upset but then she lives with the old lady and they live happily ever after.

Each of the endings I've selected broke new ground for the class in discussion. Example (a) took us straight into the familiar territory of the genre 'horror' writing I mentioned in an earlier chapter. Example (b) sends that genre up, and provoked two interesting discussions. One dealt with the endless fascination of the paraphernalia of 'frightening noises . . . black coats . . . bloody teeth', which, at the same time, was felt to be 'silly', 'not really frightening.' The second discussion was more 'literary'—many pupils felt that you couldn't 'cheat' in this kind of way. They were aggrieved with the girl who wrote this piece for setting them up to expect one thing and then letting them down. Example (c) led us directly to the 'moral' and purpose of the story. The 'morality' of the orginal story is more savage than anything the children managed. Mrs. Gertrude turns out to be a witch who without much ado turns the girl into a log and burns her.

However, example (d) provides an 'alternative' of a very different kind from any of the others. Already, in the examples referred to so far, prediction and the search for alternative routes has ceased to depend on the logic of incident and event—simply 'what happens next and why'. Here we have someone whose ending runs counter to the inexorable 'logic' of the story: 'Frau Trude is a wicked woman . . . If you go and see her you're not our child any more.' In this example that 'logic' is *judged* and found wanting—'its all roomers.' It is rejected in favour of a different morality which stresses independent judgement rather than accepting prejudice masquerading as 'good advice.'

This seems to me the real end for our encouragement of speculation and the exploration of alternatives. Our interest must lie in the development of autonomous judgement which may involve, as it does here, rejection or questioning of the 'authorial' intentions and values. If our interest remains at the level of the logic of incident, then we are simply inventing a new formalism to replace the old formalism of 'comprehension' exercises. When we or our pupils attend to a story, we are neither simply passive in the face of it, nor solely wondering what will happen next—we are engaged in an argument with it. That notion of an argument has to include the possibility of *contradiction* which is continually active and vocal in us all.

As teachers we should expect to be contradicted. This means that we need to be particularly alert to the way in which our particular emphasis, and in stories the directions we assert, can exclude contradiction on the part of our pupils. I had just finished reading the first chapter of Betsy Byars' novel *The Eighteenth Emergency* (**5**) to a class of twelve-year-olds when a girl put up her hand and said:

'You didn't read that properly.'

'I didn't read it properly.' (Teacher rather proud of his characterization and accent).

'No, you made it sound funny. It isn't funny. It isn't funny for someone to ignore you. She shouldn't ignore him . . .'

Of course, it is funny—Benjy rushes in breathless from school full of concern about the bully Marv Hammerman who is out to get him. His mother, tired and preoccupied, keeps him at arm's length. And, of course, the girl was right, it isn't funny. I'd played the scene for laughs and made that my emphasis. But, as the girl went on to explain, it depends who you are in the scene, the view you have of the events, how your view stops you seeing the other person's point of view.

I think courageous voices like this girl's often get lost in our classrooms, and they will go on being lost while teachers are tactless in handling the stories they tell and insensitive to the range of responses they stimulate in their pupils. One factor I notice over and over again in students is an incapacity to recognize distinctions in stories. They are all grist to the same mill—essentially static literary models to be 'used.'

A couple of examples may help here: Jan Mark's *William's Version* (**6**) is a story I often read to children of this age group. William's grandmother attempts to tell him the story of *The Three Little Pigs* which the four-year-old William counters with his own highly personal version—to hilarious effect. It is a marvellous story for opening up discussion about what we invest in stories, how we change them to suit our purposes, how we use them to reflect personal meaning. All those possible avenues of thought are sacrificed if you do what I find my students constantly doing, which is to read the story and then say: 'Now I'd like you to take a well-known story you heard as a small child and write an alternative version.'

F.P. Heide's *The Shrinking of Treehorn* (**7**) is another favourite for this kind of treatment. Certainly the story invites speculation and continuation—you are invited into a new adventure in the last page as Treehorn discovers that he has recovered from shrinking only to turn green. But 'Write Treehorn's next transformation' or 'Write about a day you discovered you were . . .' only encourages attention to the 'device' of metamorphosis. The 'truth' of the story lies in the localized and sharply satirical comedy at the expense of adult vacuousness. There is an emphasis to be made too which would take in Treehorn's independence and resilience in the face of adult ignorance. It is another example of children being encouraged along the 'safe' route of 'fantasy', rather than being encouraged to develop their judgement and critical sense about the world they inhabit. I have in mind here an illustration I saw recently made by a twelve-year-old of her own 'family' in which she has reinterpreted 'Treehorn.' Mother and Father argue over the head of a diminutive child—he wears every distinguishing item of bourgeois manhood (expensive trainers, the latest jogging outfit, male 'jewellery'), she is chic (tactfully coloured hair, dramatic make-up). In the background every item of the conspicuous consumption household is present—high-tech furniture, videos, home computer etc.

Illustration is obviously a powerful means of interpretation and it deserves a higher status within the context of our teaching than the time-filling excuse it so often is: 'If you've finished your stories you can draw a picture.' I shall return to the value of children illustrating their own work, but, for the moment, I want to pause to consider the place of picture books and illustrated stories in our English lessons with nine- to thirteen-year-olds.

That they have any place at all is a view which many English teachers would dispute. Instead there is a strongly entrenched prejudice that readers progress from picture books to 'real' books (without pictures). At best, there is a grudging acceptance that picture books might be permissible for the 'less able' or as a relaxation from the real business of grappling with the text. So school libraries throughout the country echo with the cry 'You can't have that if you're just going to look at the pictures.' This still goes on when demonstrably children are excited and absorbed by illustration and at a time when we have illustrators of extraordinary talent, like Maurice Sendak, Raymond Briggs, Errol le Cain.

Illustrators of the quality I've mentioned make highly sophisticated demands upon their readership, and the idea of relaxation of attention to the images they present is the last thing they intend. Equally, the children we teach are saturated by images: advertisements, TV, illustrated papers and magazines, yet little attention is given to how they 'read' these images, or (referring to my earlier argument) how they might contradict or dispute their power.

I can begin to develop my point best by describing a discussion I had recently with a group of eleven-year-olds about two picture books: *Where the Wild Things Are* (**8**) by Maurice Sendak and *Angry Arthur* (**9**) by Hiawyn Oram and Satoshi Kitamura. None of the children knew either of the books though the Sendak has been a 'cult' book for over a decade and *Angry Arthur* is a recent prize winner. I make that point simply to stress the fact that if we live in a 'golden age' of illustrated books, that good news still hasn't percolated down into the junior and secondary schools I frequent.

A more important point to mention before I discuss the reactions of the pupils was the sense of freedom and lack of inhibition in their response. Three possible factors seem significant here:

1) To show pictures to children they have to be near you—most of this group of fifteen were sitting down in front of me on the floor. After we'd 'read' the books first, we had to pass them backwards and forwards to look more closely and check out details. I find all of these points suggestive in terms of the ways we 'normally' read to children and then stand tongue-tied and inhibited by the silent, staring faces. Anyone who has worked with six- and seven-year-olds will recognize what we sacrifice in our desire for formality and routine—running commentaries, interjections, questions—for passivity.

2) Illustrations seem to me to have a way of 'equalizing' the relationship between teacher and pupil. I spoke a little earlier of the powerful emphasis and drlier of the powerful emphasis and direction even a tactful teacher can give to the text they are reading. Illustrations are much more independent of that mediation and so, as I shall try to show, they are much more open to interpretation and speculation.

3) The 'target audience' for both of these books is 'pre-school' but I don't think anyone in the group felt that they were being patronized. Indeed, the very fact that none of them, to begin with, had to feel directly involved meant that our discussion began with an air of detached appraisal, a willingness to be more critical of what the author was attempting and the methods employed.

From an adult, psychological point of view, both books deal with a child's powerful feelings of anger and aggression at being thwarted and present them working themselves out. In *Angry Arthur*, his mother's refusal to allow him to watch TV leads to a rage which grows with spectacular destructive force—destroying the world and the universe while his impotent parents stand by—until Arthur is left floating on a bit of Mars wondering why he was angry. In *Where the Wild Things Are*, the 'wild thing' Max is sent to bed and finds himself transported to the, at first, congenial and monstrous world of the Wild Things, but tired and lonely he returns to the 'real' world and the comfort of his supper.

This is not the way the children discussed the books. From the moment we began, it was a matter of argument and judgement—'you can imagine that', 'it's silly.' Indeed, I would emphasize the point that dealing with illustrations rather than a dominating text makes teacher control and direction of the flow of conversation much more difficult. Most striking is the way they keep on noticing details: significant ones like the fact that one of Max's pictures pinned up in the second frame of the story bears a striking resemblance to the 'monsters' he meets later on, or the visual jokes in *Angry Arthur*, the overturned bus advertising TYPHOON TEA and the giant cigarettes toppling out of the hoarding advertisement.

But their judgements quickly went beyond noticing surface features and began to touch on larger considerations of over-all style and intention. They were very quick to see how in *Angry Arthur* images derived from cinema are exploited. They are, after all, the generation who have grown up with 'special effects' movies, and the book might well be a collection of stills from such a film. 'It's like the Superman films' one girl remarked. Yet for all this recognition, or precisely because of it, they didn't like the book. And in registering their dislike they voiced the unresolved basic questions: 'What happens to his parents?' 'What happens to all the people?' 'It's like one of those TV programmes that just end and you don't know what's happened.' 'Fancy doing that just because you couldn't watch TV.'

It was at this point that I got rather confused about the nature of the argument which the children were developing. I put this confusion down to two causes: the first was that they began to use a terminology to make new meanings for themselves. So I didn't grasp how they were renewing terms like 'realistic' and 'imaginary.' The second cause was that I was having to *follow* an argument rather than doing what one does more often as a teacher—namely, enforcing and directing an argument.

There was a general agreement that *Angry Arthur* was more realistic. Yet, as one can see from the questions, its version of reality is challenged by judgements which emerge from the children's view that their own sense of reality—the way they would act, the questions they want answered—has been offended: 'Arthur . . . the boy in the story looks like a pretty spoiled brat.' 'It's a stupid sort of Superman story *like out of this world.*'

There may seem to be some contradictions here—why did they insist on the 'realism' of the story? The answer lies, I believe, in their constant reference to film and TV. *Angry Arthur* is 'real' in the way that films are—full of effects that look 'real.' They recognize this, while at the same time they resist the power of the images and use their own experience as a vehicle for criticism.

Where the Wild Things Are on the other hand is 'full of imagination.' It became clear that 'imagination' is not being used here as a term of dismissal. As one pupil put it: 'It's imaginary because you can imagine things like that happening . . .' This may sound like circularity but the point became clearer when she went on to say: 'In children's imagination there is monsters . . . If you're little you might be sent to bed and maybe a forest will grow and you'll be with the wild things *who don't care about you . . .*'

If *Angry Arthur* is dismissed as 'out of this world' then *Where the Wild Things Are* is clearly very much of their world. As a story it meets their most serious concerns about loneliness, lack of company, friendship and love. 'With the wild things who don't care about you . . .' implies a recognition of the need for someone who does care. They didn't ask of *Angry Arthur*: 'What happens to his parents? What happens to all the people?' because they were too literal minded to grasp the intention of the fantasy. Their identification of it with 'TV programmes that just end and you don't know what's happened' is a recognition of its incoherence, as unlike *Where the Wild Things Are*, it won't answer to their most serioius questions.

I spoke earlier of stories locating an area which we can play around with, exploit and change. I hope that it's beginning to be clear from my examples that that 'playful' activity is intimately related to the formation of judgement. It ought to be clear too that those judgements don't remain hermetically confined within the terms of reference of 'the story', nore are they based solely upon personal experience. Children from an early age are developing what I'll call a 'world-view': making judgements about and trying to make some sense of events and issues in the contemporary world. They discuss them amongst themselves, as one of my sons had when he returned home from school one day to tell me that: '. . . he and Darren had solved the Falkland islands problem . . . why didn't we have one half and the Argentinians have the other half?'

These are capacities which we should be encouraging in our pupils. The children I have just been describing have the capacity to discriminate amongst the versions of 'fantasy' they are presented with. They also have the capacity, if encouraged, to discriminate about the versions of world events and history with which they are confronted.

I followed up our discussion of *Angry Arthur* and *Where the Wild Things Are* with another picture book: *The Expedition* by Willi Baum. (**10**) Unlike the other two books, *The Expedition* has no text, so there is an even greater freedom to interpret. The absence of a text, that is, encourages the pupil to concentrate on what the story *means*. This seems to me incidentally one way of meeting the problem referred to in a report on Language Performance in Primary Schools: 'The main cause of the pupils' misreading of the story therefore might be said to stem from the fact that they interpreted what the characters in the story *said* rather than what they *meant*.' (**11**) Not, of course, that the problem is confined to primary pupils.

The Expedition in a series of fourteen pictures presents the following 'story': a gunboat arrives off a tropical island. The ship's captain spies a building on the island—'a sort of temple like in Egypt,' one pupil remarked. The captain and crew land on the island, plant a flag and then hack their way through the jungle to the 'temple'. On arrival, they dismantle it, taking down the gold carvings and removing the 'idol'. They make their way back to the beach to discover that only the hull of the ship remains. The whole superstructure has disappeared. Eventually, the captain trains his telescope on the temple and he discovers that his superstructure has reappeared there. It sits on the steps exactly replacing the temple building with the funnels smoking away. In the final picture, the crew row their ship back into the sunset with their disconsolate leader.

As with the other two stories, I was struck immediately by the attention of the pupils to the detail of the pictures, and how noticing and interpreting go together. They were taken with the planting of the flag on the beach—'he's somebody who wants to make his mark . . . like people who put flags on mountains . . .' They quickly formed a low opinion of the 'leader', and had it confirmed when someone noticed that when they go through the jungle, he takes second place behind the sailor sent on ahead to cut a path—'because he didn't want to get killed.' They were amused by how 'all the sailors look exactly the same'—same uniforms, same expressions, same actions. They noticed (I'd missed it completely) that in the dismantling picture the captain carries the 'idol' tucked under his arm.

Nor was their attention simply a matter of following up details as they occurred. On a second 'reading' they immediately cross-referenced two pictures. The first is the captain's original view of the island through his telescope—'clean and peaceful', silhouetted against a clear blue sky. The second is his view of the temple—thick black smoke pouring from its newly acquired funnels set against a lurid sunset, the island vegetation dark and in shadow. What most powerfully focussed their attention was this sense of a beautiful place spoiled and 'polluted'. Equally strong was the sense that no one had gained anything: 'I think they both lost out because the boat would have been better with the engine and the temple would have been peaceful.'

As we talked the conversation moved into more general areas of judgement: 'Sometimes people take things from other countries for museums . . . And sometimes they put horrid modern things there instead. I don't like some groups of people because they think that if they land there and stick a flag there that place is theirs. I think that people shouldn't let them take things from their own country.'

Not that the conversation in any sense represented a steady progress —no real conversation does—any more than we exhausted all the possibilities of the story. They showed no real interest in who the inhabitants of the island were, or if they still existed. How the miraculous exchange had taken place was again of little consequence. On the other hand, little unexpected side-shoots sprang from the more general discussion. The flag planting seemed to reappear consistently and at one point provoked this dialogue:

> 'It's just like the Falklands, isn't it?'
> 'How do you mean?'
> 'Well, how do you know something belongs to you and not somebody else?'
> 'You have papers and documents.'
> 'Yeah, but how do you know?'

My suggestion as we were drawing to a close that they record some of the points raised in discussion met with a mixed response. Those pupils who had been most active in discussion didn't see the need for writing anything down—'but we said all that.' On the other hand, one boy who had said nothing wrote the following:

'The story represents greed and selfishness. It is like people taking animals out of their normal habitat. There is lots of greed in this world and lots of arguments. The man in the story looked as though he thought he was very important and lots of people in the world are like that.'

It is this boy's own writing which offers the best case to the others why writing something down might be important. Here is somebody who has listened to and considered the arguments, and who summarizes them. In the process he opens up by his analogy a new line of thought. Writing is particularly suited to this function. Nor—though he'd said nothing earlier—did he mind me reading this statement to the rest of the group. He offered what seemed to me a chance to end the lesson on a deliberated and serious note while suggesting other issues for exploration.

He is certainly right about one thing—that we live in a world of argument and dispute, full of issues like the one he raises, that cannot be taken for granted and which demand solutions. This is the world we are educating these children to enter. It follows that the stories we introduce and tell them have to give them access to opinion and enable opinions to form. They belong, if they have any value at all, to that world of argument. What they promote, if we refuse to academize or anaesthetize their arguments, are the embryonic political and social views which these children are struggling to articulate.

Such a view ought also to suggest where the real 'service' lies that English might perform in the context of the whole curriculum as opposed to its frequent designation as a 'skills' area. In the context of primary schooling it would seem obvious, but even at the secondary level I would hope, for example, that the work I have just described would make a contribution to the historical thinking of my pupils. That it would give them ways of thinking about the nature of colonialism and of criticizing the versions of the world they receive. Historians tell stories, too, though it seems to be recognized rarely by History teachers. So my pupils draw pictures of castles and may, in my part of the country, make the statutory trip to Caerphilli or Chepstow, without being encouraged to ask what they represent in the colonization of a subject people. Not only the story but the *history* 'represents greed and selfishness'.

The responsiveness of these pupils to illustrations leads me to suggest further developments in the area of the visual arts, particularly as looking at pictures does not seem to have a priority with Art teachers. Amongst non-text illustrators, Mitsumasa Anno strikes me as outstanding. His book *Anno's Journey* offers a 'project' of a unique variety. It is an inexhaustible compendium of stories, running visual jokes, allusions to great paintings, tricks with perspective, literary references —all within the framework of a journey through the 'Europe' of Anno's imagination. It is where I intend to go next with the pupils whose responses I have been describing. It offers too a sophisticated version of the seeking out of routes and directions in stories with which I began this chapter. As Anno says himself: 'When a man loses his way, he often finds himself—or some unlooked for treasure. By the end of my journey, I realized that I had not set out to collect information but to lose my way—and to discover the world you will find in this book.' (**12**)

6

Children as illustrators

This chapter will be mainly devoted to the significance of illustration and its relationship to the written work of pupils—particularly those pupils who normally find writing a defeating process. How can one go about setting up such an activity and how should we assess the efforts that pupils make?

6

Children as illustrators

It was not with children in the nine to thirteen age group that I first discovered the value of illustration. I stumbled upon it when I was trying to find something which would motivate some of the fourth and fifth year secondary pupils I was teaching. The fourteen- and fifteen-year-olds that is who still have 'reading ages' of nine, and who at that age are still unable to answer for themselves the question 'why write?'

In a last ditch attempt to find something Four Commercial/Technical would or could read and to keep them quiet for two hours, I remember taking into school every single picture book I possessed. And it worked—they went through the lot from Captain Pugwash to Beatrix Potter—'There, sir, and you didn't have to shout at us once.'

Nevertheless it was still with some trepidation that I suggested that they might like to try their hand at producing a picture book —something, perhaps, that their younger brothers or sisters might like to read or that might work as a 'reader' for children lower down the school. As it is, I now count amongst my most treasured possessions the books they and other groups produced: 'Mr. Benn and the Potato Men', 'Nessie's Birthday', 'Buildings with Faces' . . .

The point I want to stress is that I am talking about pupils whose 'normal' written work—where it existed at all—was a bad joke. Work never completed, handwriting so careless and indecipherable that it could only manifest a calculated insult, exercise books which were thin, blotchy volumes of failure. In contrast to that state of affairs, what these little books demonstrated in every aspect of their production was *care*:

1) Every story was completed and the 'finish'—the look of the thing— was crucial.
2) They were all marked by extraordinary attention to detail and an attempt to make each one look as much like a 'real book' as possible, e.g. sewing the pages together, putting on hard covers, typing in some instances, making their writing bold and legible (as much like type-face as possible), even 'copy-writing' their productions.

3) They had thought very hard about the conventions of the picture book—particularly the relationship between text and pictures. Size was important too, and a lot of them had gone for the 'child-sized' format of Beatrix Potter's books and the Revd. Awdry's 'railway' series.

The success of this venture made me think very hard about what had been at stake in it for my pupils and what the distinctive elements had been that had produced this renewed effort on their part:

1) The first point to make is that the picture books themselves in such profusion had awakened or reawakened their 'aesthetic' sense. They are beautiful, often lavishly so and they make a sharp contrast with the text books and 'readers' pupils of the kind I'm describing normally have to endure. I think we underestimate to our cost the importance of the general visual environment for our pupils and, as they grow older, classrooms become more and more just boxes for learning in—there is a sharp contrast here between primary and secondary classrooms in terms of 'display': What the books produced were potential models of design and standards of excellence in execution, without which personal standards have no hope of forming themselves. If I am challenged in my use of the term 'aesthetic', then I suggest we might consider some of the 'criminal' (in school terms) activities in which these pupils engage—the elaborate care with which they decorate the *outside* of their exercise books, their bags, their desks, and, increasingly, themselves. The instinct for 'display' is all around us.

2) The movement beyond the exercise book or the folder of incomplete 'attempts' is crucial. What I was asking them to produce was a 'work'—autonomous, complete in itself, and not muddled up with a collection of bits and pieces, unrelated and disparate in their intention. I believe that this has a significant effect on the care and attention that the 'producer' brings to his or her finished product. Exercise books are for exercises and note books are the place for notes, rough drafts, trials, etc. When we view the carpenter's chair or the sculptor's carving we don't expect it to come with the sawdust, shavings or rubble which is the by-product of their activity.

3) The pupils had a clearly defined *audience*. So, from the beginning, 'how you do it' has to be thought of in terms of 'who it's for'. There is an interesting complication here, of course, because although these pupils were writing a text for children younger than themselves, their own level of competence in the language was itself in most cases the same as their target audience. It wasn't therefore a matter of *simplifying*, but rather one of finding an appropriate style or voice and doing your very best in that manner.

The stories were tried out on their target audience and I know of some teachers who have gone much further than the 'home-made' productions we attempted, seeking for a wider 'audience' for their pupils through more sophisticated forms of reproduction, even commercial reproduction in some cases. Every means we can exploit seems valuable to me for the self-esteem of our pupils. I would stress in addition the motivating and sustaining face that the pupils give each other while the work is in process. The atmosphere of the English classroom becomes much more like that of the Art room or the Woodwork room where pupils wander round, have a look at the work in progress, even *sometimes* criticize or give advice.

4) There still remains a fundamental question which I found myself asking—wouldn't just writing a story have been simpler, more apparently within their grasp? All the way along the line from conception to finished product there are choices to be made of many different kinds—choice of story, audience acceptability of the text, style of illustration, layout, size of format, 'binding', etc. Contrary to my initial expectation, the range of choices is sustaining and self-supporting. The pupil is involved in every aspect of production, and the responsibility and independence this enforces is far removed from the continual sense of 'doing things for teacher', executing their idea. Equally, there are so many things to think about that the writing is only part of a hierarchy of problems. It isn't now 'the thing you're not very good at' upon which you myopically concentrate, but it's seen within the perspective of other activities, in which you have varying degrees of skill. If within that range of problems you can solve some of them, then you strive to match the quality of those solutions in other areas. To put it another way, instead of dwelling in the lowest common denominator of one problem, they strove across the range to achieve the highest common factor.

The first link I want to make between the account I've just given and our work with younger pupils has to do with the special kind of identity the older pupils had with their stories. Through being so actively engaged in their making, their stories were their 'possession' in the fullest sense. It is possible to have this sense of possession even when the original story is not your own.

A friend of mine was teaching a 'special class' of eight-year-olds, and of the books he'd read to them, *Rosie's Walk* (**1**) by Pat Hutchins was their favourite. Everybody wanted to read it, but there was only one copy. So my friend suggested that if they made a big version of it, everybody could read it. This is what they did—pupils took on responsibility for various parts of the text (which is very simple) and individual pictures. In the end they produced an enlarged version of pictures and text in a strip which went round the walls of the classroom. So everybody could read it, but when they asked to read it they didn't say, 'Can we go and read *Rosie's Walk?*', they said, 'Can we go and read *our* story?'

I find with my own children of this age and many of the children I've taught, a related preoccupation with copying (and no 'copy' ever lacks interpretation) illustrations from favourite books, and a desire to re-write favourite stories. I take this as a measure of the profound impact certain books have and a desire to 'make those books our own'; to possess them in a very special way. It is also something which signals, in my view, the difference between the child who may be a 'functional' reader, and the child for whom reading has become an active necessity.

It doesn't seem a step too far removed from what I've just been describing to encourage our younger pupils to start thinking of themselves as book makers and illustrators. Many of the reasons why I think this is a valuable activity for top juniors and younger secondary pupils derive from my experiences with older pupils. Nevertheless the actual approach I adopt has important differences. My older pupils worked individually on their own stories. With younger pupils I tend to make this a group activity, and I give each group a story to work on. I also adopt a more systematic approach than I did with my older pupils. I'll now go on to describe the stages in order and outline the thinking behind each stage:

1) The first decision has to do with *choice of story*. For fairly obvious reasons, I look for stories with an episodic narrative, stories which move swiftly from one strongly realized scene to the next. So I avoid 'naturalistic' stories and look for 'legendary' material. In my stock of stories I have four Red Indian legends: *How White Man Lost His Eyes*, *The Story of Stories*, *The Seven Stars* and *The Legend of Thunder*. (**2**) I usually work with that number of stories because I'm going to divide my class into four groups, with eight or nine pupils in each.

2) The second stage is the actual *telling* of the stories. That *telling* is quite deliberate and I only do it once. I don't read from a copy and there are no copies around for the pupils to refer to afterwards. I think this is very important, and although I want to spare my pupils the problems of invention, I also don't want them to feel dominated by an 'authorized version'. The selection and interpretation they make is the important thing.

   Although each group works on only one story, everybody has heard the other stories—this becomes more important later.

3) I'm obviously putting a considerable emphasis on *listening*, and, contrary to what's often said, I find children of this age attend well, and have extraordinarily retentive powers and remember detail. Having assigned each group a story, this is a useful time to 'fix' the story initially—simply by getting them to retell it within the group. It's also the time to help if there are any major confusions.

4) Once I feel reasonably confident that each group is in preliminary possession of their story, I ask them to 'block' it. I usually suggest they think in terms of eight or ten pictures with an accompanying text which will carry the story.

This is the first major task for the pupils for they now have to select and establish a sequence for their own story and appraise their 'original' for its potential in terms of significant moments for illustration.

5) It's only when they've 'blocked' their stories that I usually turn their attention to how they are actually going to set about producing their 'book'. They've known from the start that it's a picture book that each group is working on and I am presuming too some background knowledge of picture books. Nevertheless, I think an example helps, particularly if you can find one in which a 'real' author has attempted to tackle the same problems they are about to face. Working with these particular stories, I usually choose Elizabeth Cleaver's *The Loon's Necklace* which is a picture book adaptation of a Canadian Indian Legend.

This is the point at which we talk together, with the aid of our example, about questions of layout, the relationship of text to pictures, text length, 'view point', and the special problems that each of the stories presents.

6) When the children come to make their books, I suggest that they take responsibility in pairs for a couple of illustrations and the accompanying text. The only important thing here is that each child has a chance to illustrate and write. It's also useful to appoint an editor who will check the consistency of the writing as it moves from phase to phase.

7) When the stories are completed we always come back together as a whole class to hear them read and shown. This is obviously why it's important that the whole class know all the stories—the whole point of this session is to invite comment and discussion about how each group has treated the story.

I want to look at one such adaptation made by a group of eleven-year-olds. The story they worked on is *The Seven Stars*. Their method of presentation is very simple. The story has been divided into eight 'frames' with an additional cover page. The illustrations are on plain A4 paper, the text is set below each picture 'caption style', and text and illustrations have been mounted on coloured sugar paper. The text runs as follows:

1) This is a story of a beautiful girl who lived a long time ago with her mother and father. She was quite a lonely girl, so one day her mother decided to teach her how to sew. She got some porcupine quills and deer skins which she made into lovely suits. She made several of them because she was lonely she went in search of brothers.

2) So she packed her bags and got the dogs and set off to the end of the world—AMERICA!!

3) She arrived and saw one big tepee. Then she saw a young boy. She said I'll take you for my brother. The beautiful girl gave him the smallest suit. He put on the moccsins and the shirt and trousers. Then she put the rest of the six suits on the six beds.

4) The six brothers came home to the tepee and saw their little brother with his new suit and one of the brothers said Where did you get that suit? A beautiful young girl gave it to me inside there are six suits for you.

5) Early in the morning the brothers set out for their hunt. The girl and the boy cooked their dinner but then a calf came running out of the forest. The little boy said What do you want? The calf said we want your sister. No you can't have our sister the little boy said. The calf turned and went back into the forest. Then a heifer came out of the forest. The little boy said What do you want heifer? We want your sister. No you can't have her the little boy said. The heifer turned and went back into the forest.

6) So a herd of buffalo was coming to trample them to Death. Then the six brothers said to the little one, save us. So the little boy fired an arrow at a solitary tree which began to grow.

7) The seven brothers and the girl climbed up the tree, half way up the brother shot an arrow and the tree went higher, while below the buffalos circled the tree and their chief rammed it.

8) They went up into the sky with the buffaloes surrounding down below. The head buffalow was chopping chunks out of the tree so it grew higher and they jumped off and turned into stars.

So far I've concentrated on describing a procedure (the way the teacher can order the activity) and the *end product* (what the children actually wrote). More important than either of these is the actual *process* in which the pupils have been engaged. It ought to be clear even from the surface disparities between each individual piece of text that this is the work of children at many different levels of 'competence'. The pupils include a number of children who find 'individual' writing a defeating process, as I described earlier. Section 2 is a case in point.

Gareth's nineteen words are a tremendous achievement. *On his own*, I have not yet seen him complete nineteen words which make sense—yet what *sense* these words make! More than anyone else he has gone beyond simple recital. His exclamation (AMERICA!! is in seven different colours in the original) captures all the sense of excitement and anticipation that he believes the girl must feel. It is also a striking piece of invention on his part—I made no such point in my telling of the story. But the exclamation is also on his behalf—an exclamation at his own success. Gareth may not be able to write very well, but he can draw dogs. His illustration for this page is dominated by the girl and two magnificent dogs straining through the wilderness with their heavy packs. He also had to draw the dogs for the person who wrote and illustrated Page 1. They dominate the foreground of that picture where the girl sits sewing outside the tepees of her tribe.

My point is that it is the communal and collaborative nature of the activity in which Gareth has been involved which has sustained him. In the *process*, there are also four important things about writing which I hope he and his contemporaries might learn: (**3**)

1) *Writing does not have to be a sedentary activity.* Teachers who favour children being 'chained' to their desks should not embark on this activity.

2) *Writing does not have to be a silent activity.* Writing nearly always involves exchange with other people, exchange of views and ideas, work in progress, successes and failures.

3) *Writing does not have to be a solitary activity.* This is particularly true for unconfident writers—Gareth wants and needs to be with his friends.

4) *Writing is never a tidy activity.* Real writing (and the manner in which these children have worked) spreads to all available surfaces, including the floor. It also involves scissors, sellotape, coloured pens, staplers and paper clips as well as pens and paper.

In other words, as I'd discovered with my older pupils, writing can be conceived as part of a range of activities which are mutually sustaining. Amongst these the opportunity to illustrate has been crucially important to Gareth. It has helped him to 'realize' something in the story. This is also true of the others. The writer of Page 3, for example, reports rather flatly, but in her accompanying illustration she remembers a detail from my telling of the story—the girl comes to a broad flowing river and on its opposite bank she sees the tepees of her future 'brothers'. The illustration includes this as part of a bold composition dominated by the river with the girl waving to the little boy on the other bank. Something similar happens in Page 8 where again there is a rather matter-of-fact narrative. The illustration here is ingenious and 'fuller' than the text. We see only the top of the tree, almost lost in clouds. Six stars are already shining brightly, but just emerging from the foliage is the last 'star' and, in the transformation, we can just see the head of the last boy.

I hope it's clear from this account that the pupils haven't just been wasting their time 'drawing pictures'. The illustrations are an essential part of their realization and expression of what the story means. That meaning can be expressed with more complexity and shaped more 'artistically' through illustration than it can through writing for many of them. Nevertheless, the illustrations have enabled them to sustain and complete a competent narrative—something which should encourage them in their future endeavours in writing.

There is a recognition too that 'meaning' in a story is more than a rehearsal of events. I am interested in why the writer of the text to Page 6 evocatively calls the tree 'solitary'—I didn't use that word. In every picture from Page 6 onwards there is the dominating presence of a single tree and it is present again as the dominant image on the 'front cover'. This suggests to me an artistic 'logic' which the children have grasped in their expression of the story. One which overrides apparent inconsistencies in the logic of events—the fact, for example, that in the first picture the girl has yellow hair whereas in the second picture her hair is black.

It would be possible, to find a place for the activities I've just been describing as part of a programme of work on 'Red Indians'. My only caveat would be that we continue to recognize the 'truth' of the representations made by these children without getting obsessed that their 'Indians' wear the wrong clothes, decorate their tepees in 'unIndian' patterns, etc.

It was reading Caldwell Cook (4) and his account, now seventy years old, of the place and value of illustration which helped me most to clarify this point. When speaking of his pupils' engagement in the mapping and illustrating of stories he says: 'We use the older form of the word, and call our thing an Ilond, to distinguish it from a piece of land surrounded by water. For an Ilond has no geographical situation. It is rather a region of faery, a country in the clouds.'

To go back to Gareth's piece of text, it would be absurd to tell him that the Indians lived in America; he probably knows that anyway. But 'AMERICA!!' (in seven different colours) is 'the end of the world'.

7

The function of poetry

This chapter is an attempt to ascribe a function to poetry and to reassert its place at the centre of the curriculum, instead of standing apologetically on the sidelines to be introduced as a light relief. The particular stress in this chapter will be upon a variety of ways in which pupils can become engaged with the words of the poems—literally 'giving voice' to their meaning.

7

The function of poetry

There can be few better places to start a consideration of poetry in the classroom than this passage from *The Rainbow*:

'. . .the teacher read on, fired by his power over the boy. Tom Brangwen was moved by this experience beyond all calculation, he almost dreaded it, it was so deep. But when, almost secretly and shamefully, he came to take the book himself, and began the words 'Oh wild west wind, thou breath of autumn's being,' the very fact of the print caused a prickly sensation of repulsion to go over his skin, the blood came to his face, his heart filled with bursting passion of rage and incompetence . . . He could not voluntarily control his attention. His mind had no fixed habits to go by, he had nothing to get hold of, nowhere to start from. For him there was nothing palpable, nothing known in himself, that he could apply to learning. He did not know how to begin. Therefore he was helpless when it came to deliberate understanding or deliberate learning . . .' (**1**)

Lawrence only has to quote one line of Shelley to make us recognize how the exclamatory note it strikes jars with the instructional routines of the classroom. Tom is left doubly confused. He is left at the mercy of feelings which he can neither comprehend or give any coherence to. Significantly too, his sense of failure with the day-to-day currency of school work which the poem interrupts is increased. He feels even more helpless in the face of the demands of 'deliberate understanding'—the mechanically argumentative discourse which leaves him convinced that 'He was a fool'.

The extremity of Tom's feelings are particular to him, but they give us a clue to the confused and confusing way in which we introduce poetry. In the very act of reading a poem we say to children: 'be moved', 'feel', 'the teacher read on, fired by his power . . .'—an invitation which is uncommon and confusing enough in the context of most schooling. Yet the next moment (I rarely observe more than one reading before the questioning begins) we're off down the track of 'deliberate understanding'. To do this is merely to stimulate feelings and then promptly to disregard them. Tom's disorientation, the sense that the last thing you can or want to do is 'explain', is, I believe, very common in children.

I remember sitting with a group of thirteen-year-olds listening to Edwin Morgan's *In the Snackbar*—for thirty-five minutes their teacher relentlessly questioned them about its subject, the author's attitude, what they felt, what they thought they would have done. Sweating and disheartened, she was convinced that they were a stupid, unresponsive class. Yet their tightlipped resistance suggested to me that they had responded only too well. Quite simply they found the poem embarrassing, arousing only too many complicated feelings of guilt and revulsion that don't emerge to order at the flipping of the teacher's response button. I thought their silence was honourable —the best response in the circumstances to glibness and the mechanization of response.

The first thing we ought to forego is this demand for immediacy of response which is the trademark of the examination room. If we are genuinely interested in the 'development of response', then the timescale for that development will have to extend beyond a myopic obsession with what can be assembled, packed and assessed in thirty-five minutes. Nor is that development within our control; as Lawrence wisely remarks: 'Nothing is more difficult than to determine what a child takes in, and does not take in, of its environment and teaching . . .' (**2**)

So poems need time—time to work upon their audience, not time to be ceaselessly worked upon. Read often and leave alone is perhaps the best advice anyone can give. Lines, odd words and phrases have a way of sticking and floating into consciousness as part of that process of fixing a poem 'by heart'. At the moment, I'm reading Baudelaire and one line has stuck with me and surfaces from time to time:

'Je suis comme le roi d'un pays pluvieux . . . (**3**)

I don't know why. I haven't made any *deliberate* attempt to learn it, but I recognize it as part of the process of knowing the poem, the way its expression becomes natural to you. Poems we might remember don't simply give expression to thoughts and feelings we already have. To have them 'by heart' is to have accommodated the expression of new thoughts and feelings.

Children, I find, are extraordinarily retentive even after just one reading, and one rule of thumb check on the impact of a poem is just to ask them how much they can remember. It's a tactful way of sharing our experience of a poem—concentrating away from 'meaning' and on the recognition of mutual enjoyment. Like my fourteen-year-old son who remarked one evening, out of the blue: 'We did a good poem at school—about ice-skating. (Wordsworth?) Yeah, that's right: "The leafless trees and every crag/Tinkled like iron . . ." It's good that bit.'

Nor do I see any harm in children of any age being actively encouraged to learn poems by heart as long as it isn't turned into an absurd classroom competition. I envy the people over sixty I meet who have a repertoire of poems they learned in childhood which haven't been subjected to analysis or criticism.

> 'Tyger, Tyger, burning bright
> In the forests of the night,
> What immortal hand or eye
> Could frame thy fearful symmetry.'

That's a verse I know so well I have no need to make any checking reference to my Collected Blake. Yet it still resists my attempts at 'deliberate understanding', at offering a discursive account. So what should we expect from a group of eleven-year-olds?

This was a question I posed some years ago to a student of mine who wanted to read *The Tyger* to just such a group. What to do after the reading? Conscientiously, she had the questions ready—give meanings for individual words and phrases, the pseudo-botanical classification of similes and metaphors. Let's abandon the questions, I suggested. But if we abandon the questions do we also abandon any attempts to enable the children to articulate their response?

It is here that I have to return to my remarks in the previous chapter about illustration: 'The illustrations are an essential part of their realization of what the story means. That meaning can be expressed with more complexity and shaped more 'artistically' through illustration . . .' So we read the poems to the class and asked them to go back to it and choose a line or a phrase and to attempt an illustration. My original intention in making this suggestion was very modest—an attempt to give more time, an encouragement to go back and consider the detail of the poem.

If I was hesitant the children were not, for the consistent characteristic of the illustrations which the children produced is firmness of intention and boldness in execution. Blake himself, writing of a child's drawings he had looked at, puts it much better: 'They are all firm, determinate outline . . . All his efforts prove this little boy to have had that greatest of all blessings, a strong imagination, a clear idea, and a determinate vision of things in his own mind.' (**4**)

Some of the illustrations are of startling simplicity—a hand outstretched, flames in yellow and red extending up from it, yet not consuming it:

> 'What the hand dare seize the fire?'

In another an elaborate interlocking pattern of spears and stars on a blue ground:

> 'When the stars threw down their spears
> And water'd heaven with their tears'

Equally striking is the way in which no child attempted what I'll call a 'naturalistic' account of the poem. Rather, what one recognizes repeatedly is an attempt to integrate pictorially the symbolism and imagery of the poem. In one, the tiger crouches as if to spring, its left foreleg held by a chain tethered to a tree. This movement of uncomfortable restraint is framed by the trees—whirls of colour and twisting branches which flame against the night sky, the whole landscape pierced by spears.

Throughout there are attempts at imposing an order and coherent design. Rubbed out in one of the illustrations is the first rather haphazard attempt—the tiger floating rather vaguely at the left of the picture. In the finished version the tiger's position has been turned to accommodate a line that takes the eye in a curving movement from stars falling from top left of the page down to the tiger which has almost emerged from a great swirling mass of flames dominating the bottom right of the picture.

The word I want to return to in trying to give an account of these responses is boldness—boldness of conception and execution. The articulation of response through an expressive rather than a discursive medium seems to have had a liberating effect. Before discussing this further I want to present two more examples which may help to clarify my point. The children involved were the same age and on both occasions we were working on a mime prompted by the ballads I had read to the class.

In my first example, it was *Sir Patrick Spens* we were dealing with, and we had reached the point where the king despatches a messenger to Sir Patrick carrying the orders for the ill-fated voyage. We were working in a large assembly hall and the children had remained grouped together for their opening riotous court scene:

'The king sits in Dunfermlin town
Drinking the blude red wine . . .'

Yet now the two boys playing the messenger and Sir Patrick altered the whole note of the proceedings. In the ballad, the sense of impending doom is expressed in Sir Patrick's *reaction* to the letter—

'The next line that Sir Patrick read
The tear blinded his ee'

—the messenger is just a messenger. In a moment of total absorption the boys focussed on the messenger—his conflict—not by working up emotions, but by an act of extraordinary restraint. Their boldness lay in using the whole space of the hall—two isolated figures—for a long moment the messenger stood watching Sir Patrick—

'. . .was walkin' on the strand . . .'

and then slowly he began to walk across his empty space until finally he delivered the message. What can I say other than for these minutes time stood still. Through their intense concentration and use of space they made us feel every resistant step of the way.

My second example concerns *The Wife of Usher's Well*. We had reached the point where the three babes have made their ghostly return to their grief-stricken mother:

> 'She spread them a table on a milk-white cloth
> And on it she put cake and wine.
> Come and eat, come and eat, my three little babes,
> Come and eat and drink of mine.'

The group were handling this return very formally and ceremonially —the mother seating each child at table. Then I noticed another figure in the background: a girl scurrying about sweeping and dusting, making a fire. 'Who are you?' 'I'm the servant. Somebody has to tidy and do the housework.' There is no servant in the version I had read, but here again we have that spontaneous realization of a possibility to be presented. Life—domestic reality—has to go on and this action of the girl, her absorbedly getting on with her tasks offered a revealing counterpoint to the strange unreality of the main action. Here invention presents the emotional truth which the ballad explores—the mother's attempt to act as if life had not gone on because she cannot bear the loss of her children.

It's a curious contradiction to be making so much of occasions which for the children concerned were so impermanent—neither my illustrators nor my mimers made the reflections I have made on their actions. So what did they learn? I can't help thinking back to the likely outcome of having pursued the 'twenty questions approach' to 'The Tyger '—how much less likely boldness and absorption would have been the words to characterize the faltering and brain-cracking session it would probably have turned into. The 'deliberate understanding' of such an approach makes learning and its relative difficulty so *conspicuous*. In contrast, I hope my examples demonstrate learning which is *inconspicuous*. So much learning which goes on in school is learning only to forget. But *understanding* grows inconspicuously—it's so pervasive that we don't even regard it as learning. So my assessment of the examples I've quoted is very much a matter of saying what was at stake for these children at that given moment. I'm trying to disentangle moments of growth, not checking off items of memorized information.

To go back to Tom Brangwen, what we recognize is a child who is panicked by 'deliberate learning' and then assailed by the emotional impact of the poem. The result is that he can think only of himself and his own incompetence. What the shift to an expressive act seems to have allowed the children to do is to forget themselves and to concentrate on the subject matter. The obvious care which has been lavished on the illustrations, the absorbed deliberateness of the mime is the best indicator I know of feeling which is authentic. As Dewey remarks: 'the spontaneous in art is complete absorption in subject matter that is fresh, the freshness of which *holds and sustains emotion*; staleness of matter and obtrusion of calculation are the two enemies of spontaneity of expression.' (**5**)

In stressing the connection between poetry and learning, I'm anxious to assert that we don't have to apologize for poetry's presence in the classroom, pulling it out from time to time to sugar the pill of routine learning. The seriousness of the poetry I've referred to and of the response it evoked ought to suggest too that we don't have to be apologetic in our selection of poetry. 'Poetry is fun!' Well, it is sometimes, but not to the exclusion of all poetry other than slim collections of verse which assemble knowing little jokes, wisecracks and wry anecdotes about 'growing up' and 'adults and their funny ways'. Poetry isn't always 'fun', any more than poets are always clowns and comedians.

If we go back to the years when children's learning is most inconspicuous and purposeful—the pre-school years—we may rediscover a function for poetry which is inseparable from learning. My four-year-old's poetry book is called *The Mother Goose Treasury* and this collection of rhymes, songs, ballads, puns, riddles and tongue-twisters is just that—a treasury. The body of poetry from which it is selected is the most comprehensive 'language development programme' that we have, tailored by the collective wisdom of the historical community.

As a programme, it has aspects which are severely functional, not the least of which is that it helps the learner to effortlessly retain many of the basic patterns of our grammar. More significantly, in view of its long term implications, it promotes attention and listening. George Ewart Evans records the following Suffolk saying: 'The lil' ol' boy sat on his father's knee while he wor a-telling him a story. And he kept lookin' at him *as though he wor a-pickin' the words out of his mouth.*' (**6**) I can think of no phrase which quite so vividly conveys the beginning in the child of a sense that words *mean*—that they make and transform experience. Such attention (all teachers will bear me out) is not *natural*. It can only result from the regular experience of having something meaningful to attend to. Yet that attention is essential to learning.

My son's friend, James, has just started school. When he came to play recently I was sitting in the garden reading and he joined me with a book he'd found and sat down next to me 'reading' it. Displaying great tact he recognizes that books are important to us, and while he's with us, he does what we do. Yet if we try to read to him or tell him a story, he quickly loses interest or wanders off. He is not dull, nor is he incapable of absorbed play. It is not so much that he loses interest but rather that interest never begins—the expectation of meaning, which is what I mean by 'attention', isn't evident yet. It isn't that he is anti-pathetic to stories and poems, rather, largely through lack of experience, he doesn't distinguish them from the 'noise' of general discourse.

Having had your attention drawn, you can then begin to make sense of your experience and begin to distinguish sense and nonsense amongst the linguistic 'noise' which is the medium we and young children inhabit. Why is there so much 'nonsense' in nursery rhymes? It can only be that by encountering 'non-sense' we begin to appreciate what makes 'sense' in language and what does not. Underneath much apparent 'nonsense' too we find the severest laws of causality operating:

> 'An old woman went to market and bought a pig,
> Pig had four legs
> But pig would not go.
> Well, says the old woman, what shall I do?
> She went a little further and she calls to a dog,
> Dog, dog, bite pig,
> Pig will not go
> And I should have been home two hours ago
> But the dog would not . . .

'Making sense' can, of course, mean more than internalizing the logic of causation through listening and repetition. The gallery of monsters which haunt nursery rhymes is not primarily meant to terrorize children to make them good. Even at two years old, the pressure came from my son and *not* me to 'Read Giant!'

> 'Fee, fie, fo, fum
> I smell the blood of an Englishman:
> Be he alive or be he dead
> I'll grind his bones to make my bread.'

You have to learn what to be afraid of—passing through the stage of being at the mercy of your generalized fears and anxieties to that of fearing a specific creature. Emotions, that is, become more real, more known through the definition they achieve in metaphor and dramatization.

Not that the human emotions recognized in these verses are limited to fear and anxiety. Indeed much poetry written for children seems anaemic and censored compared with the range of emotional life present in these rhymes. And though they have a didactic function —linguistic rules, conceptual rules, rules for living—there is a strong critical and subversive strand. It is through nursery rhymes, for example, that children first encounter the possibilities of satire:

'Oh the Grand Old Duke of York he had ten thousand men . . .'

They permit too what in ordinary discourse would be unspeakable and impermissible to the young child—expressions of rage, anger, undiluted plain speaking:

'I do not like thee, Doctor Fell,
The reason why I cannot tell
But this I know, and know full well,
I do not like thee, Doctor Fell.'

Though often the feelings expressed are much more ambiguous:

'Trip upon trenchers, and dance upon dishes,
My mother sent me for some barm, some barm
She bid me tread lightly, and come again quickly
For fear the young men should do me some harm.
Yet didn't you see, yet didn't you see
What naughty tricks they put upon me:
They broke my pitcher,
And spilt the water,
And huffed my mother
And chid her daughter,
And kissed my sister instead of me.'

I have made this digression because I wanted to search out some time when poetry mattered in the lives of children, and because I think as teachers we've lost sight of the function of poetry. However, it is unfair to blame teachers—rather we might consider the sheer abnormality of poetry continuing to be read in the classrooms of a society in which poetry has lost its function. It came as a shock recently to me to read the following account:

'In modern times poets have had a greater impact on popular culture than novelists: there are more published poets than authors of literary prose in the Arab countries today, and public readings by poets consistently attract mass audiences in settings ranging from rural villages to sprawling and sophisticated capital cities.' (**7**)

And for a schoolboy's poetry to provoke the following reaction is incomprehensible:

'The next day Darwish was summoned by the military governor, who insulted and threatened him. Darwish left the office shaken: 'I wept bitterly because he concluded by saying, "If you go on writing such poetry, I'll stop your father working in the quarry."' (**8**)

I offer these examples as an essential reminder that somewhere in the contemporary world poetry is alive—capable of appealing to a popular audience and giving voice to its fears and aspirations, critical and

subversive in its expression. They suggest too horizons towards which
we might be directing the gaze of our pupils if our commitment to their
understanding the many cultures which have penetrated our own
means anything at all.

But we don't have to look that far afield for poetry which is alive. We
have in the British and American folk song tradition just such a
resource. My reasons for making this suggestion are two-fold. First,
there is an obvious connection between the significance of nursery
rhymes in the development of the very young child and the part that
folk song and poetry can play in the development of older children.
This is only to reassert the continuity which existed in the traditional
community. Second, it is the most effective way I know of demonstrating to children that poetry is not *special*—neither the prerogative of
a peculiar élite or handed down from on high on tablets of stone from
some 'poetic' heaven. Folk song and poetry speaks of the lives of men
and women: of their workplace, their sports and pastimes, of how their
aspirations have been met or thwarted, of the comedies and tragedies
which make up human experience.

Such an emphasis seems to me to place poetry, where it truly
belongs, at the centre of the curriculum. I've suggested on a number of
occasions the importance of validating children's experience; of
enabling them to tell their story. Yet the very language they use and
add to is the result of a collective endeavour—of men and women
telling their stories, making their poems and songs. Convincing our
pupils that they are not dumb and inarticulate has to go hand in hand
with a recognition that their forefathers were not the silent instruments
of 'experts' and those who 'knew better', nor constantly at the mercy of
'events'. Rather they were sceptical and irreverent in the face of authority and they sought for reasons and causes which underlay the
day-to-day reality of their lives.

The best models I can suggest to anyone interested in exploring this
area are the Radio Ballads which Charles Parker produced for the
BBC—many of which have been re-issued on record by Argo. It is
precisely the collective endeavour I spoke of earlier which Parker
captured in programmes like *Singing the Fishing, The Big Hearer* and *The
Ballad of John Axon*—each with its own unique mixture of anecdote,
reminiscence, song and music.

That mixture is the most powerful and effective medium I know for
initiating children into the public world for which their education
should be preparing them. The history and geography they learn will
only be of any use to them if they are encouraged to understand that its
roots lie in a multiplicity of personal stories and in the complex lives of
communities—flourishing and in decline. No amount of instruction in
'life skills' will avail unless they have been encouraged to attend to the
voices of men and women who have real skills and experience to impart

and the wisdom which goes with them. As for poetry, what can it mean, unless they recognize its dependence on the living idiom of men and women, on their attempt to give shape and form to their experience:

'What a feeling you have when you get off the shed; you've got the engine, you've got the control of it, and what a feeling—I'm cock of the bank, there's nobody can take a rise out of me now, she's mine. Come on, me old beauty, and off we go. The moon's out and the countryside —it's lovely. On we go, what a feeling—she answers to every touch. Some more rock on, lad. Yes—it's grand.'
(Jack Pickford—Driver, speaking on *The Ballad of John Axon*).

I'll conclude this chapter as I began it with some suggestions about classroom practice:

1) Let the emphasis from the start be on *performance and interpretation* and not on *talking about* the poem. The most useful collections of material I know for working in this way were not made for English lessons, but for Music lessons and they are the first two volumes (*Voices* and *Moods and Messages*) in John Paynter's series *All Kinds of Music* (OUP). (**9**)
The emphasis here is on the way in which we can convey meaning through attention to sound and rhythm and how we can convey mood and tone through voicing and simple instrumental techniques.
One way of starting with younger pupils is to work on 'sound poems'—collective performances of single words and groups of words. See in this connection the two poems *Thunder* and *Bonfire Night* in Peter Warham's *Electronic Music in the Primary School*. (**10**) In this area I've found the poems of Edwin Morgan invaluable—they demand performance, for what else is there to do with the *Loch Ness Monster Song, French Persian Cats Having A Ball* or *First Men on Mercury*? (**11**)
I see no reason why such an approach should end in the primary school. One of the first ways I've introduced Shakespeare's poetry to children is by asking them to 'set' the songs from *The Tempest*. I've told them the story and we've usually dramatized the shipwreck. The next stage—as in the play— is to explore the island and its inhabitants—an island, you'll remember:

'. . .full of noises,
Sounds and sweet airs that give delight and hurt not.'

2) 'The human voice is the most sensitive instrument we have for communicating ideas.' Infant teachers recognize this both for their pupils and themselves. There is no sense in their classrooms that singing, chanting and reciting means putting on special 'musical' or 'poetic' voices. I can see no reason why the years between infancy and the onset of broken voices should be lost. Nor can I see any logic which allows a valuable half hour or hour to be given up to hymn or assembly practice while dismissing song from the classroom.

With the younger pupils, we might make a start with the repertoire of 'tall-story' songs like *The Derby Ram, Paddy and the Whale* and *Who's the Fool Now*:

'I saw a maid milk a bull
Every stroke a bucketful
I saw the man in the moon
Clouting off St. Peter's shoon'

These are all songs which encourage on the spot improvisation and embellishment. It would be refreshing too to hear classrooms and assembly halls enlivened by the range of celebratory and seasonal songs we possess beyond the hoary old Christmas favourites—wassail songs, May, Easter and Whitsun carols (the collection on Topic Records, *Frost and Fire*, is an invaluable resource in this respect) (**12**).

3) Teachers who are interested in pursuing the documentary value of song will find that much of the initial research has been done for them if they consult the collections of songs and contemporary records edited by Roy Palmer—*The Valiant Sailor, Poverty Knock, The Painful Plough*. (**13**) They will also find the catalogue of Topic Records and their leaflets on Folk Song in English and in the Humanities a useful starting point.

4) It ought to be clear by now that I think we should dispense with those poetry lessons which concentrate on the 'comprehension' of single poems or pairs of poems to 'compare and contrast'. I'm equally dubious about 'thematic' approaches in which the poem is reduced to the status of illustrative material. The clue to an alternative form of organization and linkage lies in the organizing principle inherent in one of the forms of poetry I've emphasized in this chapter—the ballad. As the ballad scholar G.H. Gerould has remarked, one of the striking features of the ballad form is: 'the discontinuous method by which the whole story is presented to us . . . The events burst out in a series of flashes each very sharp and each revealing one further step in the action . . . There is unity because the flashes are all directed on what is essential to our imaginative and emotional grasp of a quite simple situation'. (**14**)

The best example I can give of employing this principle is a ballad-drama I developed with a group of second year secondary pupils based around four songs: *All Things Are Quite Silent, Lowlands Low, The Ship in Distress, A Fair Maid Walking*. The songs sustained a narrative—a man is pressed into the Navy—we focus first on his wife's reaction—we move to his life at sea—eventually they are reunited but test each other out. It is a story as old as the Odyssey (which I was reading to the class at the time.) We filled out the drama with contemporary material: an opening scene where the pressgang make their proclamation, a letter from a sailor on board one of the receiving ships which provokes the despair of *Lowlands Low*, an account of a battle at sea. The songs sustain a narrative, but more importantly they act upon each other to unfold an emotional development. So we move from the contained grief of:

'All things are quite silent, each mortal at rest,
When me and my true love got snug in one nest
But a bold set of ruffians they entered our cave,
And they forced my dear jewel to plough the salt wave.'

to the despairing:

'I'll cut away my bonny hair
Lowlands, Lowlands, away my John,
No other man shall think me fair
Lowlands away.'

Next we meet a different kind of intensity in the man's life which denies reflection:

'You seamen bold who plough the ocean see dangers
    landsmen never know
The headgear gone and the masts a-tottering
No tongue can tell what we undergo
Through the blustrous wind and the great dark water
Our ship went sailing all on the sea . . .'

And we end with the moment of recognition:

'He put his hand into his pocket
His fingers being both long and small
Drew out the ring that was worn so thin,
When it she saw, well she down did fall.'

To quote Gerould again: 'a folk song tells a story with stress on the crucial situation, tells it by letting the action unfold itself in event and speech, and tells it objectively with little comment or intrusion of personal bias . . .' I can think of nothing further removed from the account of poetry as manipulation of feeling and response with which I began this chapter.

5) In making so strong an emphasis I hope I won't be misunderstood as being too exclusive. I believe that one should try anything, and of all areas poetry is the one where we could afford to take a few risks. When I first started teaching and knew nothing about 'poetry for children', I naively read to a class of twelve-year-olds sections from

Christopher Logue's translations of the Iliad, since reprinted as *War Music*. (**15**) An equally naive art teacher I mentioned it to, used the sections we'd read as the basis for a sequence of Iliad paintings.

In front of me now I have a new anthology of 'poems from many cultures' *I like that stuff*. (**16**) I applaud its range: historically from Sappho to Brecht, geographically from Hungary to Zimbabwe. We need many more like it in our classrooms for us and for our pupils to browse in. Indeed, browsing through an anthology of Eskimo poetry, I found the following statement which might well have stood as the epigraph to this chapter:

> 'Songs are thoughts which are sung out with the breath when people let themselves be moved by a great force, and ordinary speech no longer suffices.'

8

Telling the children

This chapter devotes itself to discriminating about the kinds of stories we choose as teachers to bring to the attention of our pupils. What kind of 'response' are we interested in evoking in them? What is our interest in content, or the 'issues' present in a story? What other criteria are being employed? The second half of the chapter contains suggestions as to sources of short story material. What kind of stories might we be looking for as an alternative to reliance on the class novel?

8

Telling the children

Reading a collection of tales from South West Africa recently, I discovered that the tribe amongst whom the tales had been collected had three different words for a 'story'. These words translated meant 'telling of what happened long ago', 'telling the news' and 'telling the children'. I want to concentrate on the third of these meanings in this chapter—what kind of stories shall we tell children and how should we conduct the telling?

First, however, there is something that needs to be said about that second meaning—how do we 'tell the news' in our society? Here is one account that I find helpful. 'If the art of storytelling has become rare, the dissemination of information has had a decisive share in this state of affairs. Every morning brings us the news of the globe and yet we are poor in newsworthy stories. This is because no event any longer comes to us without already being shot through with explanation. In other words, by now almost nothing happens that benefits storytelling; almost everything benefits information . . .' (1)

We still use the word 'story' to describe loosely the 'news' that we read in the papers, listen to on the radio and watch on television, but usually what we are being offered is 'opinion': 'no event . . . comes to us without already being shot through with explanation'. Judgement and selection of 'stories' has been made in advance and this reveals itself in overt interpretation, and more powerfully through the style of representation. Amongst the features of that style we might point to the personalization of presenters, reporters and expert commentators, and an equivalent lack of emphasis on the background to events or the participants in those events. 'News' is a closed and discontinuous narrative to which neither those whose 'stories' are being manipulated nor their audience can gain access, interrupt or criticize. The heroes and stars of these 'stories', those whose presence provides continuity are the presenters and reporters—the opinion makers and formers themselves.

Charles Parker, whom I mentioned in the previous chapter, offers a very different version of how people's stories might be told. He saw the centre of his programme research as 'conversations' with participants in events: 'never an "interview" is conducted.' As for the role of reporter, this he felt entailed 'communicating a belief in the capacity of the person he is with to speak well and tellingly of his experience of the subject at issue; and this usually in the teeth of all the preconditioning that our society engages in as if to convince ordinary people that they cannot express themselves adequately.'

I think that most teachers would agree that one of their aims is to convince their ordinary pupils that they can express themselves adequately. What we have to guard against when 'telling the children' is that we don't engage in the same dissemination of 'opinion' and manipulation of our audience which characterizes 'telling the news'. What I'm concerned about are the stories which teachers choose to bring into the classroom—both the reasons for their choice and what they choose to do with them. This choice of 'teaching stories' is something which they have within their control: what children choose to read for themselves is another matter. What teachers do with stories can affect that choice. At the same time it would be naive not to recognize that children's fiction is part of a commercial operation that identifies a large market to be exploited and 'needs' that can be created amongst children. The children's book industry has become increasingly skilful at exploiting that market with a publicity machine rich in film, TV, cassette and video tie-ins, personal appearances, pop-ups, cut-outs, mugs, posters and tee-shirts. As with the associated popular music and clothing industries we are talking about the world of fashion and not story —'fantasy' is out, 'realism' is in—until the next change.

What strikes me about the books which get chosen for classroom use is their sheer 'opinionatedness'. It is as if, as with 'news', there was a repertoire of issues and concerns which it was necessary to get across to our pupils. Books which present these issues are especially favoured and books which don't 'fit' are either rejected or receive draconian treatment. So, in a recent review of children's books where you find teachers commending books to other teachers, I made a list over a couple of pages of the following issues: 'a major work of fantasy located . . . in the *inner city*; the saga is *political* both internally, in its *theme of conflict, invasion and survival*'; 'a book that questions *sex roles* as well as warning against *nuclear war*'; 'other novels using the concept of a *stratified and highly* controlled society are . . .'; 'Is this 'about' *vivisection, or eating meat, or is it an allegory of Auschwitz*?' (**2**)

If we were to change just one word in my earlier quotation from Walter Benjamin, we would get near to the circumstances which prevail in many classrooms: 'no *story* comes to us without already being shot through with explanation'.

In the same review, another teacher-reviewer concludes his commendation of Robert O'Brien's *Z for Zachariah* as follows: 'The diary form makes compulsive reading and underlines the humanity of this important novel, which should form the basis *for exploring the issues that surround its very controversial subject matter'*. Our reviewer then goes on to list *Things to Do* (the other dominating criterion behind the choice of books for the classroom—the more 'things to do', the better the book):

'As a *pre-reading* exercise make a Survival Priority Game. On each of 20–30 pieces of card write one different activity of post-holocaust survival, e.g. find fresh water . . . Groups of pupils then arrange these into columns of top, mid-term and long-term priority and discuss with other groups their final conclusions. (Good to use with *Lord of the Flies* too!)

Make a chart that shows the order in which things first become, and will increasingly become, irreplaceable in the valley.

Draw a map of the valley, labelling points where key events might have occurred'.

The interesting thing about this list—and though it's not exhaustive, I take the items to be priorities in teaching—is that it concerns itself neither with 'humanity' (either in the book or its audiences) or 'exploring the issues'. The book asks us to think about what for most children and adults is unthinkable. I take it too that it can hardly fail therefore to arouse powerful and largely unresolved feelings and anxieties. Not least because, in addition to its nuclear scenario, we are asked to follow the threatening relationship which develops between a man and a defenceless young girl. What the pupils are offered are time-filling diversions which neither meet these feelings or inform them. What are they supposed to make of the Survival Game—that the post-nuclear world will be some kind of jolly adventure, when they know that even to think of survival is a lie? Such an approach seems to me destined to leave children feeling even more powerless in the face of events and even more 'disinformed' than they were to begin with.

I well remember meeting a class of third-formers who had spent half a term reading *Z for Zachariah* along with the by now almost obligatory reading of Peter Porter's *Your Attention Please*. The general mood seemed to be one of depression and dispiritedness. This was not simply a result of what they had just read. It spoke too of the blunting and exhaustion of 'response' which results from *The Silver Sword* and *I am David* in the first year, *Walkabout* and *My Mate Shofiq* in the second year, and the prospect of Wilfred Owen in the fourth year.

Novels of the kind I've been referring to and the associated classroom treatment they receive seems to me to place a double strain on children. On the one hand they call upon their audience to 'identify with' or 'empathize with' the individual psychologies that populate such stories. While, on the other hand, the way in which they are 'taught' increases the emotional stakes still further by importing a background of 'issues' and 'situations' about which you're meant to feel deeply or become impassioned. It seems to me a recipe for stimulating the sensations rather than educating the emotions and, like all forms of 'sensationalism', it creates jaded appetites which can only be aroused by more extreme stimulation. Of course there are other kinds of novels, but it's interesting to see how the teacher-reviewer I quoted earlier deals with one of them. The novel in question is Jan Mark's *Thunder and Lightnings*: 'Quite a long novel which, in my opinion, needs a brisk treatment if it is to succeed . . . Girls might complain a bit that there are no strong juvenile female roles'. The question of 'success', of course, only matters in the context of the class-reader—as well as writing a novel which is too long, Jan Mark has also, on her own admission, written a novel which doesn't have 'a plot'. I'm more interested by the implicit judgement that a novel only works on a simplistic notion of 'identification': 'no strong juvenile female roles' so the girls complain, whereas it does work with the 'less-able' because they 'sympathize' with Victor. What do we want stories to do—simply to reflect and confirm the views children already have of themselves? Are we to presume such a limited sense of their own shared humanity amongst young adolescent girls that they can recognize nothing in the story of a friendship between two boys? And what of the two mothers in the story, aren't they strong female roles? The real issue at stake is that Jan Mark has simply failed to write the ideal first-year class reader—it's too long, too literary ('the dialogue requires practised handling'), there are insufficient (stereo) types to identify with, and it's a bit thin on 'issues' ('Making new friends, Victor's school report, and library research on the aeroplanes mentioned' is a bit tame).

So what other kinds of narrative might we be bringing into the classroom? I'll offer some examples and consider their implications. Earlier, in passing, I mentioned *The Silver Sword*—still, along with *Stig of the Dump*, amongst the top ten classroom novels in top junior and lower secondary classes. Although it is anthologized and easily obtainable, Brecht's ballad *The Children's Crusade* has no such currency. In four or five pages, Brecht tells the story of a group of refugee children wandering through the debris of the Second World War, hoping to

> '. . .reach a country
> Where there was peace.'

They don't, and they disappear unnoticed just as their wanderings go on unnoticed in the midst of the conflict. Though the subject is harrowing, its treatment is quite unsensational, and though individual children are mentioned there is, in novelistic terms, no 'psychology':

> 'A girl of ten was carrying
> A little child of four.
> All she lacked to be a mother
> Was a country without war . . .

> . . . A girl of twelve, a boy of fifteen
> Had a love affair
> And in a mined farmyard
> She sat and combed his hair . . .'
> 'But love could not endure
> Cold wind began to blow:
> And how can saplings bloom
> When covered deep in snow?'

You'll notice too that 'questions' don't have to be imported from outside, but are immediately and disconcertingly there in the narrative. Instead of opinions we have to consider authoritative judgement:

> 'Let no one blame the poor man
> Who never asked them in
> For many have the will but have
> No flour in the bin.'

What we have, in other words, is a narrative mode, which seems to me to contradict both the manner and intention of the kind of novel I was discussing earlier. Novels in which the

> '. . .situations are hastily assembled to
> Excite the customers to rage
> Or pain. The audience
> Thus becomes voyeurs. The sated
> Sit next the hungry.' (**3**)

In this sense 'telling the news' and 'telling the children' are indistinguishable forms in our society. They both *direct* attention and questions away from the causes which underlie the great events and issues which govern our lives. Brecht's *simplicity* both concentrates and commands attention. He is neither arousing feelings or importing explanations which get in the way of the audience's capacity to interpret.

It is significant too that commentary appears in the Brecht as powerful *generalization* with an almost proverbial expression:

> '. . .And if they stole let no one blame
> Who never bade them eat. . .'
> '. . .For many have the will but have
> No flour in the bin. . .'
> '. . .How can saplings bloom
> When covered deep in snow. . .'

Just as events are important because of the *point* that they make: they are not there simply to illuminate the personalities of the participants:

'There was a school for penmanship
And teaching did not cease.
On the broken side of a tank
They learned to spell out peace'

Much of the literature we offer to children seems to work in the opposite direction, placing a high value on the individual case history—in some cases to the point of eccentricity (think of those rebellious, 'non-conformists', hyper-sensitive and self-conscious child heroes and heroines who haunt the pages of so many American children's books).

Consider the differences, for example, between *Z for Zachariah* and the folk-tale from South America *After the Fire*. The folk-tale opens with an account of internecine warfare between two tribes—warfare that has become self-vindicating and self-perpetuating (no one can remember the causes) and which absorbs all human energy. The two tribes fight each other to a stalemate, each side matching the other's attempt to gain an advantage. This continues until—and it's not clear which side starts it—a great fire breaks out, which destroys all the land except for two survivors, a man and his wife. This part of the story is sketched out in about three hundred words. *Z for Zachariah* leads us straight to the individual case history whereas the opening emphasis in the folk-tale is on causes and events which are beyond the control of the individual, but in their origins are *typically* human.

The second half of the story deals with the survivors and their confrontation with Sararuma ('an evil spirit who hated all mankind'): 'As they stood together, they saw what seemed to be a red flame twisting across the blackened earth toward them. It was Sararuma in his red flame cloak.

'Do you like your new home?' Sararuma taunted.

'Yes,' said the man, and his wife nodded.

Sararuma's flaming cloak paled and, at their feet, grass blades, a vivid green, pushed through the ashes.

'You think this won't all happen again? You want to live to see that?' screamed Sararuma.

'We want to live,' said the wife.

Sararuma's cloak paled again and through it the man and his wife could see new leaves covering the charred trees.

'You're on your own,' said Sararuma.

'Not forever,' said the man. 'We shall have children' added his wife. Then a cooling wind rose which swirled about Sararuma putting out his pale fire and blowing away his words.'

Again characterization and individual psychology are insignificant. We don't ask ourselves what clothes are they wearing, where will they find water, how are they feeling? The generalized presentation denies the response 'how would I feel if I were them?' What matters is *what* they say and our sense that *it is possible* to say such things. Unlike *Z for Zachariah* we are not being asked to imagine a future the very thought of which we should refuse. Rather we are being asked to consider how men and women can act to make a future by refusing a language which preys upon their fears, their sense of helplessness and their cynicism.

I can summarize my argument so far by quoting some more remarks by Walter Benjamin about storytelling: 'Actually, it is half the art of storytelling to keep a story free from explanation as one reproduces it . . . The most extraordinary things, marvellous things are related with the greatest accuracy, but the psychological connection of the events is not forced on the reader. It is left up to him to interpret things the way he understands them, and thus the narrative achieves an amplitude that information lacks.'

I'm interested in Benjamin's point about amplitude as it relates to what I said earlier about simplicity. Neither the Brecht nor the folk-tale could be simpler, in fact as texts they're a good deal simpler than the special texts designed for the 'younger reader' or the 'less-able' pupil. Such simplicity calls upon the greatest artistry. It also offers to us as teachers the possibility of a literature of common access to the variety, experience and intelligence which our pupils possess. It is not a literature which attempts the impossible task of simplifying things down to their level, but which, to paraphrase Benjamin, leaves it up to them to interpret things the way they understand them. It might be a way too of counteracting the boredom which besets those of our pupils who are fluent readers faced by the sheer 'thinness' of so many of the novels on offer in the classroom. At twelve I'd already read *Animal Farm* and *1984*, and I've taught pupils who have done the same, or who already consider themselves to be adult readers. If they are still reading children's novels, then they'll be reading books like Jan Mark's *The Ennead*, Jan Needle's *A Fine Boy for Killing* or Russell Hoban's *The Mouse and his Child*—novels which are not easily mediated in the classroom because they are 'long', literary, and demand a sophisticated readership. I see no reason why they or their contemporaries who are still functional readers should spend their time trying to deal with novelistically packaged 'opinion'.

So where should we look for a body of stories to read to nine- to thirteen-year-olds—stories, in James' phrase, 'whose main care is to be typical, to be inclusive'. Here are some suggestions and some further thoughts:

1) Obviously, in 'folk-tale' we have one of the richest sources of the kind of narrative I've been describing. I don't rely upon them or recommend them out of any sense of nostalgia. As Brecht says 'the people has no wish to be folk. It is the same as with folk costumes, which were once worn for working or going to church in but now serve merely for parades.' Folk-tales have suffered badly from that

kind of nostalgia and an associated stress on the fantastic and quaint elements. Equally I'm unconvinced by the arguments for their psychologically therapeutic value. I'm more convinced by an argument which would assert the value in education of an accumulated body of wisdom. In many respects they seem to me to be like an immensely old grandparent who is an endless fund of story and experience. The experiences may seem far removed from 'childish' experience, but we'd be making a mistake in thinking that children are only interested in their own or other children's experience (a mistake I believe many children's writers make). They have an eye, particularly at this age, to an adult future. I remember in this connection Ursula's reaction to her grandmother's reminiscences:

> 'the grandmother's sayings and stories . . . accumulated . . . and became a sort of Bible to the child. And Ursula asked her deepest childish questions of her grandmother.
> 'Will somebody love me, grandmother?'
> 'Many people love you, child. We all love you.'
> 'But when I am grownup, will somebody love me?'
> 'Yes, some man will love you, child, because it's your nature. And I hope it will be somebody who will love you for what you are, and not for what he wants of you. But we have a right to what we want.'
> Ursula was frightened, hearing these things . . .' (**4**)

What these narratives abound in—love, luck, coincidence, chance and providence, the sheer unpredictability of experience and the mysterious precariousness of life, goodness and evil—all these things are self-evidently intelligible to children and provide a way of asking questions about the contradictions of the world they grow up in.

As for sources, I think the teacher needs to browse in the great classic collections like Grimm and Afonseyev (the great Russian collector). I very much like Italo Calvino's *Italian Folk Tales* and Sybil Marshall's collection *The Everyman Book of English Folk Tales* (not least because she also records a family ghost story, one of the most frightening I know). When looking for stories outside the European tradition, I think one has to be careful. I distrust the compendiums—'A Thousand and One Tales From Round the World' so favoured in primary schools, which look and read like encyclopaedias. The idiom of the retelling is also very important and I'm never quite sure why Red Indians and Aborigines, for example, are given an impossibly poetic diction. In this respect, one is often better off going to the folklore or anthropology section of a library and looking at the collections where the author's intention has been a faithful record rather than a 'writing up', and then making one's own versions.

What I do know children enjoy are those stories which are drawn from the various 'trickster' traditions: Ananse, Old Man, Coyote, Maui, with their irreverent ingenuity, jokes and escapades—all determinedly 'unmoral'. I recommend in this connection Harold Courlander's *Ijapa the Tortoise*. What they do resist is the mediation of these stories as little childhood tales from the childhood of the race like one extraordinary collection I found from the Cameroons where the tales were interrupted by cosy disquisitions by a Cameroon's mother (civilized, of course) to her children. The tales themselves were mainly concerned with cannibalism, incest and the replacement of old wives by young ones which made it all the more extraordinary.

What we need to guard against in our presentation of these stories is the kind of creeping progressivism and the tendency to 'third-worldize' which dominates contemporary discussion of these cultures. The Aboriginal inhabitants of Australia, for example, strike me as a deeply philosophic people with an intensely developed sense of themselves in relationship to the environment and universe they inhabited. In the light of their stories, traditions and culture there seems to me a good deal of 'educating' that needs to be done about our own self-concepts (which children share)—what we mean, for example, when speaking of ourselves as 'advanced'. Advance which generally has been and continues to be at the expense of these peoples. Such discussion might provide a real grounding for multicultural education, and an alternative to the intellectual tourism which the media provides.

There are other less well-known traditions that we might explore. The fantasy tales collected in *A Thousand and One Nights* are well known but each of the countries of the Middle East and Central Asia has its own distinctive tradition. In the Arabic and Islamic world there is a distinctive vein of 'teaching stories', often parable and fable-like in form, concerned with 'enlightenment' and 'illumination'. Idris Shah is not the most trustworthy of sources but he offers a place from which to start.

2) Coming nearer home we have to hand the stories—often dependent on folk-tale and legend—reworked and remodelled by our two greatest writers Shakespeare and Chaucer. In Chaucer, I'm thinking of stories like Chantecleer and Pertelote, and the folk-tale which forms the centrepiece of *The Pardoner's Tale* (an excellent dramatized version of which is reprinted in David Holbrook's *Thieves and Angels*). For Shakespeare's tales I think we lack a good modern version for younger children—Lamb is impossible which leaves the David Kossoff retellings, or Ian Serraillier's *The Enchanted Island*. Again, in the absence of much else, one might as well depend on one's own retellings.

Once with a first-year secondary class, I remember telling the Holinshed version of the *King Lear* story, then telling the Shakespeare version. We made an attempt at dramatizing the first part of the story and then we acted in class the opening scene of the Shakespeare—Lear's division of the kingdom and his rejection of Cordelia. What struck me then (this was a 'mixed-ability' group) was how problems with the unfamiliarity of the language evaporated once you were familiar with the story. 'Why did he have to write it this way?' is a familiar complaint from older secondary pupils and they have a genuine problem in not being able to see the wood for the trees (particularly when the species and genus of every tree is being laboriously explained to them). Wouldn't an early familiarity with the stories help with this problem and, if we're thinking of long-term continuity in our teaching, don't we have to lay down the foundations of enjoyment in advance? Many years later I met one of the girls who had been in that first-year group and she told me how the memory of being told the King Lear story had lain dormant until one day in the sixth form there was the moment of recognition when she opened up *King Lear* not for the first but for the second time.

I was equally struck by a student telling the Faust story to a group of thirteen-year-olds, basing it on the Marlowe version —struck, that is, by the reaction of one pupil who said immediately the story was finished: 'That's the best story I've ever heard . . . and I'll tell you why. When you're at school your parents and your teachers tell you to work hard, learn all you can, get your exams, so you can go to university. Then look at all the trouble you get into!' It's an eccentric response to Faust's aspiration after knowledge but it's very definitely someone responding unpredictably to a story —'interpreting things the way he understands them'.

We might make as our aim then in these middle years of schooling that we make some of these great stories the common property of our pupils and I'd add to the ones I've already mentioned names like Prometheus, the Bible stories, and so on. So much of our enjoyment of literature in the later years of schooling and in adulthood depends on allusion and reference, and there is a world of difference between meeting these stories for the first time as an inexplicable footnote to a text, and accumulating them to have their force reawakened in the moment of recognition I spoke of earlier.

3) Tolstoy as a writer and educationist was deeply interested in stories which relate 'to the simplest feelings of common life open to all'. He wrote many tales in this spirit drawing upon the Russian tradition of fable and folk tale. They are always marked by directness of address: 'It once occurred to a certain king, that if he always knew the right time to begin everything; if he knew who were the right people to listen to and whom to avoid; and above all, if he knew what was the most important thing to do, he would never fail in

anything he might undertake'. (*Three Questions*) Simple and direct certainly, but this ought to stand as enough of an indication that his concerns are always for (to use one of his titles) 'What Men Live By'. I share the preference of most children for writers who declare their interests from the start, rather than smuggling them in.

There is a selection in paperback called *Fables and Fairy Tales* (**5**), and though it's out of print, it's worth hunting for *Twentythree Tales*. One of my favourites for younger children is *Ivan the Fool* which has a list of comic characters—Imps, lazy brothers, a Devil—and which I once dramatized. Showing the script to my headmaster, he advised me after he had read it that it 'smacked of Communism'. I defended myself by explaining that it was Tolstoyan as opposed to Marxist communism, but it just shows you how careful you have to be.

For older children, I advise particularly *God Sees the Truth, But Waits* and *How Much Land Does A Man Need*, and, for something outside the fable mode, two 'adventure' stories based on Tolstoy's experience: *A Prisoner in the Caucasus* and *The Bear Hunt*.

4) I've had occasion to mention Brecht frequently in this chapter. His plays find their ways into school and so occasionally does his poetry. His stories have been difficult to obtain, but the position should be eased by the appearance of *Short Stories (1921–1946)* (**6**). For older children I particularly commend *The Unseemly Old Lady, The Heretic's Coat* and *The Angsburg Chalk Circle*. For younger or older children it is worth consulting *The Anecdotes of Mr. Keuner*—a series of sardonic fables and anecdotes—and particularly one entitled *If Sharks Were People*:

'. . .If sharks were people they would have enormous boxes built in the sea for the little fishes . . . Of course there would also be schools in the big boxes. In these schools the little fishes would learn how to swim into the shark's jaws. They would need geography, for example, so that when the big sharks were lazing about somewhere they could find them. The main thing would be . . . moral education . . . They would be taught that the greatest and finest thing for a little fish is to sacrifice its life gladly, and that they must all believe in the sharks, particularly when they promise a splendid future . . .'

The issue raised here, of course, may be too controversial so perhaps better not to follow it up with discussion! If you're lucky, your class may smile their understanding as the fable developed, as a group of ten-year-olds did that I read it to.

5) Tolstoy's prophecy of the 'art of the future which relates to the simplest feelings of common life open to all' hasn't been realized. We've yet to see our Aesop or La Fontaine of the twentieth century, though we still have them. But I'll conclude by mentioning two stories which in very different ways demonstrate that it can still be done. One is Reiner Zimnik's children's story *The Crane*; the other, and it's not typical of his work, is Heinrich Böll's short story *The Balek Scales*. In ten pages, Böll presents the emergence of one of those simplest feelings, and one so persistent as to be timeless—the sense of injustice amongst hardworking people at being exploited. How it is realized, grows into outrage and revolt and is defeated by force:

'My grandfather's parents had to leave the village, and the new grave of their little daughter; they became basket weavers, but did not stay long anywhere because it pained them to see how everywhere the finger of justice swung falsely. They walked along behind their cart, which crept slowly over the country roads . . . and passers-by could sometimes hear a voice from the cart singing: 'The justice of this earth, O Lord, hath put thee to death. And those who wanted to listen could hear the tale of the Baleks von Bilgan, whose justice lacked a tenth part. But there were few who listened'.

9

Drama and adaptation

This final chapter looks again at pupils involved in acts of interpretation—this time working as their own scriptwriters and dramatists. The emphasis is on the practical organization of these activities inside the classroom.

9

Drama and adaptation

One of the things I noticed when I first began teaching was the readiness with which children were prepared to read plays in the classroom. No matter how bad the material or how incompetent the readers, even the most recalcitrant classes seemed prepared to sit it out for lesson after lesson. I used to hope for the plays to be longer so that the blessed calm would be extended and because there seemed to be something approximating to interest—there would be the squabble for parts, the looking on ahead for when you came in, the nudge in the stomach for people who came in late or slowed things down. This interest seemed to be inexhaustible even into the fifth year where scarcely literate students stumbled their way through weary old 'favourites' like *Hobson's Choice* and *An Inspector Calls*.

How to explain the appeal? To some extent it must have to do with the sheer novelty of not having to follow, listen, be interrogated or write, and instead, however perfunctorily, being called upon to be active. There is something special too about a whole group of children engaging in an activity which binds them together. A sense quite the opposite of the individual exposure involved in that pointless activity 'reading round the class'. Then, there is the whole peculiarity of taking a part and the odd relationships it sets up—saying words to the person you are sitting next to as if you were his father and he was your son, or finding that for thirty minutes you are 'married' to that girl across the other side of the room.

The problem—and I don't think it's gone away—was finding decent material, particularly for younger pupils. Furthermore, one was looking to build on the enjoyment and make it more dramatically active. At the same time, there were the very real constraints of time and space in the classroom or the cutlery-laden hall, with the pressing need for a play which had parts for everybody.

These were the kinds of experience that led me to the conclusion that one way of developing the interest and meeting the problem was for us to try and make our own plays. My first attempts in this area were tentative. One obvious expedient which presented itself was to encourage dramatized readings of appropriate parts of some of the stories and novels we were reading in class. With younger pupils, a dramatized reading of the Court scene in Mordecai Richler's *Jacob Two-Two and the Hooded Fang* is a case in point. The scene depends upon dialogue, as does most of the novel. It has a small number of strongly defined parts: the Judge, Jacob, Louis Loser his defending counsel, the prosecutor, the foreman of the jury. At the same time the jury, who chip in at regular intervals, can be expanded to include every other member of the class. I inveighed earlier against the pointlessness of reading round the class and the way it pressures unrehearsed, unreflective and decontextualized reading. I would like to warmly recommend that it be replaced once and for all by thoroughly prepared and rehearsed readings in the context of performance.

But could we write and perform our own plays, and if we did, what kind of drama were we going to be involved in? None of the children I've taught have been theatre-goers. Drama for them means television drama: plays, but particularly situation comedies, children's series like *Grange Hill*, and action series like *The Professionals* or *The A Team*. Anyone who has laboured through compilations of TV scripts like *Conflicting Generations* will have recognized the conventions which govern this kind of drama. It is a director's rather than a writer's medium —powerfully visual in its use of techniques like close-up, cutting, juxtaposition of images, and so on. As a model for children's use, it isn't very helpful. Left to their own devices, 'doing a play', children will attempt to imitate the drama they've seen, but understandably the techniques don't transfer. (Children making their own television is a different matter, though in my experience they need to unlearn most of the 'techniques' they've observed.) So we end up with those attempts at 'doing Grange Hill' where the children impersonate to varying degrees of success, while at the same time failing to 'be themselves'.

At the same time, children are not naturally 'actors', any more than they are naturally 'writers'. Some of them are splendid mimics with a disconcerting ear and eye for mannerisms and peculiarities. They also can display a gift for caricature—the heavy fathers, railing mothers and no-good, cheeky children who litter many an improvization. These characters and the stereotypical situations they lock into often become routine—it's a natural tendency to stick with what you can do well. Here again, the apparently 'naturalistic' models they derive from TV are a powerful influence—that jolly, fastmoving, colloquial manner of say, *Minder*, which seems so 'realistic'.

These are some of the considerations that have led me to believe that for classroom purposes we need an alternative to 'realism'; an alternative, that is, to a drama whose main intention is to create the illusion that we are watching ordinary unrehearsed events. The other day I was watching a class of second formers dramatizing in the classroom the *Holy Thursday* poems by Blake. There were no props, no costumes, no space, no real separation between 'players' and 'audience'. The second poem opens:

> Is this a holy thing to see
> In a rich and fruitful land
> Babes reduc'd to misery . . .

One pupil had brought an apple for consumption at break-time and this was commandeered along with the waste-paper basket. So we began—a pupil stands before a group of 'babes', huddled together and watchful. They watch her polish the apple, examine it and then discard it into the waste-paper basket, which then becomes the object of a mad scramble amongst the 'babes'. As they do, so a new character walks past and pauses, carefully she takes from her pocket all her change. She systematically sorts out the large from the small change and then tosses the pence and halfpence to the 'babes':

> Babes reduc'd to misery
> Fed with a cold and usurous hand?

What conclusions might we draw from this?

1) The pupils are not intent upon 'making up' or trying to create an illusion. They are involved in an act of interpretation, an enactment of meaning.
2) With economy and directness, they use the limited resources to hand to concentrate attention 'to the point', and in doing so call upon the spectator to adopt an attitude of inquiry and criticism to the incident. There is no 'characterization' to divert the spectator's attention from this point.
3) The action itself has that marvellous fluidity which dispensing with 'realism' conveys—one action unfolds from the other and so provides its own commentary.

I want to turn now to an example of a written adaptation which seems to me to share some of the qualities I've just listed, while introducing some additional factors for us to consider. This is the opening scene of the adaptation of an Afghan folk-tale *Melon City* made by a group of third-year juniors. I've deliberately chosen an example made by a group who were not experienced in this way of working. To begin with, here is the opening of the story which was read to them:

'The ruler of a certain city one day decided that he would like a triumphal arch to be built, so that he could ride under it with all pomp, for the desirable edification of the multitude. But when the great moment came, his crown was knocked off: the arch had been built too low.

The ruler therefore ordained, in his rightful wrath, that the chief of the builders should be hanged. Gallows were prepared, but—as he was being taken to the place of execution—the Master Builder called out that it was all the fault of the workmen, who had done the actual construction job.

The king, with his customary sense of justice, called the workers to account. But they escaped the charge by explaining that the masons had made the bricks the wrong size. And the masons said that they had only carried out the orders of the architect . . .' (**1**)

Now, here is the first scene of the play:

Melon City

Narrator: A long long time ago in a market square in the town of Melon City. There sat in the middle of the square an old tramp who told the story of Melon City. One day five little children sat around the old tramp and asked how Melon City got its name.

Tramp: It all happened a long long time ago in our city. The King of Isteven wanted to build a triumphal arch to ride through in all his glory through the city of Isteven. He called for his bricklayers to build the triumphal arch.

King: Send for the bricklayers and all his men with him.

Narrator: So they started to design the plans. A few weeks later . . .

Bricklayer: Your Majesty, the triumphal arch is ready!

King: Well done m' lads! Well done! We'll try it out first thing tomorrow morning. Guards! Guards! Come quickly, Come quickly!

Guards: Yes m' Lord?

King: Go and tell the people of Isteven city that I will be coming into town tomorrow morning to try out the new arch.

Guards: Yes m' Lord.

Narrator: And so, off they went to tell the people about the King's arrival. The next morning as the King was going into the city . . .

Guards: The King is here! The KING is here!

Crowds: Ohhhhh! The KING is here!

Narrator: As the King approached the triumphal arch on horseback he realized the bridge was too low but there was nothing he could do now. BUMP! His crown wouldn't fit through the low arch. His crown fell to the floor and he nearly went with it.

King: Ouch! You silly arch. Whoever built this arch too low will be hanged. Send for the bricklayers.

Bricklayers: Your Royal Highness it wasn't our fault we only took orders from the brickcutters.

King: Send for the brickcutters.

Brickcutters: Your Royal Highness it wasn't our fault we only took orders from the brickbuilders.

King: Send for the brickbuilders.

Brickbuilders: Your Royal Highness it wasn't our fault we only took orders from the cementmakers.

King: Send for the cementmakers.

Narrator: Well, the King got so fed up in the end, that he told all the people involved to get out!

King: Get out, Get out, I've had enough!
Narrator: The King thought and thought THEN . . .
King: Quick, quick send for the wise old man of Isteven . . .

This certainly seems to me to have the fluidity and economy of action which I spoke of earlier. What it largely depends upon is the children's employment of a narrator. I've known many teachers who try to persuade their pupils away from the use of a narrator, arguing that it is a clumsy device dramatically. In naturalistic drama it may be, but here it seems perfectly appropriate and successful. The aim of the children is to get the story (and its point) over as effectively as possible. They show themselves (unlike some of the story-writers I've discussed) to be wholly in command of that story—at the beginning they know its middle and its end. That command shows itself in the way they transform the story, the way they dispense with the rather laboured irony of the original. They do this by 'presenting' the multitude 'edi-fied' (in one line) and they 'show' how justice works, as we literally watch responsibility being passed down the line. In Brecht's words, they narrate the story 'by vivid portrayal, always knowing more than it does and treating its 'now' and 'here' *not as a pretence* . . . so as to make visible the knotting-together of the events' (**2**).

The children's resolution of the problem of dramatization points us in the direction of forms quite different from the 'naturalistic'. Forms which include the use of a narrator, characters who speak direct to the audience, a 'presentational' as opposed to an 'illusionistic' portrayal of character and event, a minimal use of costume and props. These are all forms common to Classic Drama, our own Medieval dramatic tradition, Shakespeare's theatre, Chinese and Japanese Drama, and in our own century the theatre of Brecht. In the production of Hamlet I watched last night, it seemed to work that Claudius should tell us directly of his innermost thoughts. Nor did it jar that immediately Hamlet should, within earshot of Claudius, tell us of his plans for the King.

Two further points:

1) The form of dramatization the children have chosen does not de-pend upon them being 'actors'. An effective performance of this little play does not depend on a gifted minority who can 'impersonate' or get inside a character though it may depend on other skills they could be taught to develop like swift ensemble playing.
2) The act of interpretation I've pointed to in both these examples suggests a way of enacting the meaning of stories far more profitable with children of this age group than a more discursive approach. To put it simply, why do they need to discuss and give examples of 'irony' when they can show it?

It may be helpful now to look more systematically at this approach to dramatization. So I'll look at a play scripted and performed by a group of ten-year-olds. This group had had some experience with the kind of ballad mime I referred to in chapter 7. In the weeks preceding this particular piece of scripting, we had also rehearsed and performed a play of the Japanese *kyogen* tradition—*The Bird Catcher in Hell* (**3**). Kyogen, unlike the classical *No* tradition, are farces. They display many of the features I described earlier. The manner is presentational: characters announce themselves and tell the audience where they've come from and where they're going. Narration is crucial: the chorus supplies the context for action, gives us the characters thoughts, describes the action which is often mimed by the characters. I had wanted to introduce the class to these forms, but even here they took matters into their own hands. To appease the King of Hell, Kiyoyori, the Bird Catcher, offers to show his skill:

> 'I will catch a few birds and present them to you . . .'

Then, as he mimes, the Chorus describe what happens:

> 'To the bird-hunt,' he cried
> And suddenly from the steep paths of the southern side of the Hill of Death
> *Many Birds came flying* . . .'

And come flying they did, in the shape of paper birds made and cast by the Chorus, rather pleased at the way they had found of intervening directly in the action.

The class wanted to do more. It seemed to me that the time might be ripe to see if they could apply the skills and techniques they had developed on a play of their own. As to choice of story, I had read a good many of the Grimm's stories to them, so I looked there for a story that was compact in its action, but which was large in its subject and its potential for treatment. The story I eventually chose was *Godfather Death*.

I read the story to them once. That was the only reading and they never saw the text. This says something perhaps about the power of the story and their retentiveness but I certainly didn't want them to be encumbered by the text. What they remembered and what they could make of it was the important thing.

So we began immediately—the whole class—going over what we had remembered, and in the process we blocked out the main episodes in the story, fixing the main events and the characters, inventing in some places, rejecting in others. Obviously, the play we had been working on affected decisions. The idea of a narrator came up very quickly and this led to discussion of a chorus and what it could do, just as we talked about how the characters might present themselves. After a seventy-minute session we had arrived at four main episodes, and I split the class into four groups, each responsible for one episode.

The actual writing took another seventy-minute session. My main function here was editorial. They all knew the main lines of the story and the conventions we were working within. Nevertheless practical problems arise about internal consistency within the whole play and questions like where one episode ends and another begins. These are problems for them to discuss and my role was to bring groups working on adjacent scenes together to hammer them out. When there was agreement on the final script I took it away to type it up.

One phase of the operation was over, but new decisions and interpretations had to be made as we moved into rehearsal and preparation for performance. This rehearsal time took one whole school day apart from the half hour at the end of the day for the performance—we worked through breaks and lunchtime. The making of large blocks of time for intensive activity of this kind seems crucial to me. It would be possible to achieve an end result working in a more fragmented way, but one runs the risk all the time of enthusiasm and energy being dissipated. I believe strongly that it is important for children to get used to meeting realizable deadlines. I think it's equally important for schools to organize time according to the nature of the activities engaged in—the performance arts like drama and music suffer badly in this respect and get pushed out into the extra-curricular boundaries of the timetable. What these children were involved in was not *extra* but essential to their learning. It was for them, and not part of a public relations exercise to impress others, which is the case with so much school drama. As for this vexed question of time, within the secondary context, no one expects the games department to spread its ninety-minute matches over three thirty-minute sessions scattered through the week or the science department to complete experimental work in thirty-five-minute blocks. No more then should this be the expectation of pupils and teachers working in the performing arts.

So what kind of things were we doing during the day? First there was the question of music. We had used music when performing the kyogen and I had explained that the band of musicians would be present throughout the performance to accompany the action. So one group worked on their own to prepare the music, using wooden blocks, glockenspiels and recorders. We were not using costumes, but the characters playing God, the Devil and Death thought they should have masks to make them distinct from the 'human' characters, so these had to be made. The major topic of discussion, however, was how we would do the final scene where the Devil shows the doctor the candles of life. My teacherly instinct was not to bother but the class weren't satisfied with that. We discarded various suggestions like using real candles (teacherly thoughts—wax on carpets! insurance against multiple burns!) Then one of the chorus pointed to the solution staring us in the face. The candles are of various sizes. Our chorus ranged in height from about four feet to five feet six inches. The chorus could become candles by the simple expedient of standing up and wearing candleflame headdresses.

All this may sound chaotic, but the success of the enterprise depends on the teachers recognizing that they have now taken on a directorial function. There is no real problem in keeping children occupied if they have real occupations—I can rehearse the chorus while God, the Devil and Death are making their masks; while the chorus are making headdresses, I can attend to another group. It is important to remember too that children can act independently. It had never occurred to me, for example, that all the characters apart from the Chorus would want to learn their lines—but they did.

By three o'clock that afternoon we were ready to perform in the classroom to the parallel year group. I have a tape of that performance which conveys the atmosphere much better than the script. The concentration which the performers managed to keep up against the background noise of classes 'working quietly' either side of us. The hiatus while the 'town crier' struggled with the school bell which was almost bigger than she was. The improvisations away from the script by the Father who was determined to demonstrate his hard lot. But here is the script which does tell at least part of the story of that day:

Godfather Death

Chorus: A poor man had twelve children. He worked night and day to get them stale bread because it was the cheapest they could get.

Father: (sad music throughout) Oh, I have to work so hard for my children, and with another baby on the way, it will be almost impossible to live, because we have hardly any bread, I must find someone to look after him if we are to live out our lives any longer. Someone who will be a godfather for a lifetime.

Chorus: As the man walked down the winding dusty road he was weary. The sweat ran down his face. 'What will he do? He hasn't a godfather.' He sees a very faint figure in the distance.

(God, the Devil and Death are arguing. God approaches the Father).

God: I am sorry. I could not help overhearing—I will be godfather.

Father: Why do you want to be godfather?

God: I am good and honest. Your child will be the same as me. I am God.

Father: No, you give to the rich and take from the poor. You are no good, go away.

God: So, I am not suitable. Very well.

Father: What shall I do?

Chorus: (music) Beware, the Devil comes.

Devil: I overheard too. Let me be godfather.

Father: Why should I let you be godfather?

Devil: I'll make him rich and evil—I mean good, for I am the Devil, didn't you know?
Father: You are bad. You must go away.
Devil: You will regret this.
Father: I won't get anyone.
Chorus: (music) Beware, Death comes.
Death: I overheard too. I am sorry, let me be the godfather.
Father: Why should I let you be the godfather?
Death: I'll give him a good job, make him rich and powerful, and bring him up well. I am Death.
Father: You take lives equally. You may be the godfather, if you take care of the child.
Death: Oh, I will. Thank you so much, I am grateful.
Chorus: No good will come of this.
(Music).

*   *   *

Chorus: The boy grew into manhood in the comfort of death and on his sixteenth birthday . . .
Death: Now you are getting older you will be wanting a job. So as a present I am going to give you a magic herb—to give you the power to become a famous doctor.
Son: But where can I find the herb when I need it?
Death: Come with me and I shall show you.
Chorus: (music) So Death led the boy down to a wood where they walked for a long time until Death stopped.
(Music)
This is the herb, you can only cure the person if I am standing at the head of the bed. If I am standing at the foot they will die.

*   *   *

Chorus: It was a peaceful market day in the town where the doctor lived. Dogs sleeping, flies buzzing, sun shining brightly, and people idly chattering.
Flower-seller: Would you care for some fresh roses, sir?
Passer-by: Why, I believe I will. Thank you my good lady. You look very happy. Why do you smile so, if you'll pardon my asking?
Seller: But haven't you heard of this brilliant young doctor. He's just cured my son of what other doctors said was an incurable illness.
Passer-by: Nay, for I am a stranger to these parts—this doctor must be terribly good at his profession.
Chorus: The passer-by told his friends of what this woman had said and his friends told others, and word eventually spread across the country. And then the King fell ill, and the doctor was summoned to the palace.
(Music)

*   *   *

Princess: Can he be cured?
Doctor: I shall see—please leave the room.
Chorus: And the doctor thought 'The King will die. What can I do, he must not die. I know, I shall turn him around and he shall live!'
(Having turned the King, he gave him the herb and he recovers instantly. Music)
Death: You have tricked me. You went against my rules. I will let it pass just this once but next time I won't let it pass.

*   *   *

Town Crier: (with bell) Here is an important message from the King. The Princess, his daughter, is very ill. Whoever can give her life may marry her.
Chorus: As soon as the doctor heard this he went to the wood and returned to the palace with the herb.
Doctor: I will give your daughter her life.
Chorus: Though the doctor saw Death standing at the foot of the bed still he longed to have the Princess for a wife.
(Doctor turns and cures the Princes)
Death: You have disobeyed my orders. You shall be punished, come.
Doctor: Where are you taking me?
Death: You shall see. You shall see.
Chorus: Death led him into a cave dim and damp and dripping with water.
Death rolled a rock away to reveal a secret passage.
Death: These are the candles of life. The big ones are for babies, the medium sized ones are for married couples. The small ones are for old people and some babies.
Doctor: I suppose that big one's mine.
Death: No, that little stub is yours.
(Music)
Doctor: No, not that one . . . Light another one for me.
Death: No, that's impossible. Once that one goes out you die.
Doctor: Light a big one from the stub.
Death: Very well.
Chorus: But Death wanting his revenge purposely knocked the candle down.
And it went out immediately.
(Music)
The doctor fell to the ground, dead.
He had fallen into Death's hands.

The reader will recognize that this is a more sophisticated production than *Melon City*, but as a piece of drama it shares all the features I tried to bring out in my earlier comments. Obviously it has been influenced by the kyogen model, in the use of chorus, etc, but that dependence is not slavish, any more than their dependence on the actual story. They have been scrupulously faithful to its main line, but all their 'inventions' serve to point up its meaning and emphasize its significance. None of the following lines occur in the story:

> 'The sweat ran down his face.
> 'What will he do? He hasn't a godfather'
> 'The boy grew into manhood *in the comfort of death* . . .'
> 'And the doctor thought
> 'The King will die.
> What can I do, he must not die.
> I know I shall turn him around and he shall live'
> Death led him into a cave
> Dim and damp and dripping with water.
> Death rolled a rock away to reveal a secret passage.'

Always, when they invent, they go for an idiom which is concrete and direct. The flower-seller episode is completely invented, and although in some ways the most 'naturalistic' scene, it too demonstrates a grasp of the special idiom, quite unlike ordinary speech, that this kind of drama demands.

I'm very interested in this special idiom and to take the point further I'd like to look at another piece of dramatic writing. The following extract is one scene from a class dramatisation of the Achilles story by first-year secondary pupils. It is mainly the work of one boy who was withdrawn from the group from time to time for 'remedial' English:

Patroclus: Please, Achilles, I beg you to lend me your armour and horses, and let me lead your men.
Achilles: I might let you. But why should you dress up and fight as me? You might be killed. You are my friend, and I don't want you to be hurt.
Patroclus: I want to save the ships and Greece. The Trojans will think you have come back into the fight, and they will flee.
Achilles: Alright then Patroclus. But you must promise me one thing: don't go right up to Troy. There will be too many soldiers there for you to fight, and I don't want you to get hurt.
(Patroclus takes Achilles' armour, and shouts in the direction of the Trojans.)
Patroclus: I will fight you till I drive you back to your own city. But by then there probably won't be any of you left.
(He leaves, and there are sounds of increased battle).
Achilles: I wonder if Patroclus is keeping his word. Oh why did I promise that I would not fight? Why did I promise? Oh this damn world. It goes hard all the time in this world. Hurry up, Patroclus. I wonder if he has driven the Trojans back. Why did I let him go? My God, who is making that noise? It stands out from all the rest of the war-sound.

(Enter a soldier, panting.)

Soldier: Patroclus! Patroclus! (Then, as he sees Achilles, falling back in amazement.) My lord! Then . . . if it was not you I saw just now, it must have been Patroclus!

Achilles: What's wrong, soldier?

Soldier: Well, Patroclus came out charging, we followed. He was like a lion, he drove the Trojans right back to Troy; he was like a bear, he charged at them . . . My Lord! What is the matter?

Achilles: Nothing . . . carry on.

Soldier: Mighty Achilles, Patroclus was killed by Hector, the Trojan prince, in a great battle. It was a horrible sight. I was keeping guard on the prisoners while the others were fighting. The noise was so tremendous you couldn't hear yourself think. Well, I was looking around, and in the middle of the battle I saw Patroclus and Hector fighting—not like the other warriors, but real fighting. I was astonished, but glad really, because Patroclus was defeating Hector, but then a great disaster arose. Patroclus was moving to his feet when his helmet came off. Hector drew his sword and stuck it in Patroclus' head.

Achilles: Oh why did I let Patroclus go out to fight, oh why?

Soldier: My Lord, it was not your fault. It was his choice to die as a man or a servant, so he chose that he would die as a man.

Achilles: I know that, but I hate myself for it. I should have gone out to fight. I will go out there now and kill Hector. I will kill him to pay him back for what he has done.

I shall take this piece of writing as an opportunity to pull together the various threads of the argument that I've been developing about children, stories and writing throughout this book. It was Tolstoy who remarked that 'The principal skill of the teacher in teaching language . . . whereby we can guide children in their writing of compositions consists *in setting subjects*' (**4**). What is this boy's 'subject' other than the story of Achilles? A 'subject' conceived in these terms is more helpful I believe than any amount of well-intentioned work on beginnings, endings, atmosphere, plot, characterization, description, etc. This schematic approach reminds me of the way I was taught to 'plan' essays at school, with beginnings, middles and ends. Yet what we wrote about seemed to be of little significance. Indeed the titles we were given were essentially interchangeable.

This pupil very much has an 'idea' which gives coherent shape to his writing. That idea is not abstract, a set of formulae to be applied, it is concrete, defined by the contours of the episode he is reworking which starts with Patroclus' request and ends with Achilles' movement into action. He knows every step of the way that he is going. The interesting thing is the way in which within the overall shaping conception the pupil can attend to *his* ideas or perhaps, in the case of this writing we can say that he can attend to the *ideals* which he obviously finds so powerfully appealing in the story.

In chapter 4 I spoke of writing in which there was a dislocation between personal knowledge and expression. Although the subject here seems far removed from his personal experience, I would argue that he has located in that subject some of his greatest personal concerns; friendship, loyalty, honour, tact at someone else's grief, dignity in suffering. On the one hand they exist in the vigorous child life and language of the playground: 'I might let you . . . by then there probably won't be any of you left . . . Well, I was looking around . . . I was astonished, but glad really . . . I will kill him to pay him back . . .' But they exist too in a vigorously imagined adult world which can't be expressed in the idiom of the playground:

'Oh why did I promise that I would not fight? Why did I promise? Oh this damn world. It goes hard all the time in this world.'

'It was his choice to die as a man or a servant, so he chose that he would die as a man.'

Thinking of the later years of secondary schooling, here is someone who should have little difficulty with Shakespeare's dramatic method nor, having written a scene like this at eleven, should he have any difficulty with what is humanly at stake in, say, Act IV, scene 3 of *Macbeth*. That is, of course, if anyone lets him read and perform Shakespeare. As part of his maturing, we witness this pupil trying to imagine what maturity of judgement would sound like. As he searches for that voice, might we not be best meeting those needs with the maturest expression we have in our English language?

Postscript

Reflecting on the writing of his own pupils, Michael Armstrong remarks: 'It seems clear from such instances that child art is neither uncontrolled or pre-rational, but displays in a striking, even irresistible manner, the early life of reason'. I like that phrase, 'the early life of reason', and I applaud his use of it in answer to those who characterize children's learning and self-expression as 'spontaneous, happy-go-lucky, and slapdash'.

'Reason' is on the side of the children, it needs to be asserted. They are the people who display care, persistence and discipline, and who strive to make sense of 'learning experiences' which are demonstrably 'unreasonable'.

In this book, I have tried to show in a variety of guises 'the early life of reason' at work in some of the children I have taught — sometimes achieving expression, sometimes defeated. Many of them are attempting to do a great deal with small means which requires on our part a greater attentiveness to what they do achieve, lest we miss its inner logic and its expressive contours.

This leads us to conclude that the *basic* requirement for the development of 'the life of the reason' through education is that the teacher does not hold his own thought and learning separate from his attempts at prompting learning and observing its progress in others.

References

Introduction
1 *Bullock Revisited*, A Discussion Paper by HMI, DES, June 1982.
2 Wordsworth, William, *Preface to Lyrical Ballads*, 1802.
3 Holt, John, *How Children Fail*, Penguin, 1976.
4 Hadley, Eric, 'The Conversation of the Classroom', *English in Education*, Vol. 14, No. 3, 1980.
5 Pinch A. and Armstrong M., *Tolstoy on Education*, Athlone Press, 1982.
6 Bullock Revisited, *op. cit.*

Chapter 1
1 Hadley, Eric, 'The Beaver Mentality and the Commodity View, *Use of English*, Spring 1978.
2 Wordsworth, William, *A Reply to Mathetes*, 1809.
3 James, Henry, *Autobiography*, Princeton University Press, 1983.
4 Paustovsky, Konstantin, *Story of a Life*, Harvill Press, 1966.
5 *A Language for Life*, HMSO, 1975.
6 Tolstoy, Leo, *Childhood, Boyhood and Youth*, Oxford University Press, 1969.
7 Crossley-Holland, Kevin, *The Battle of Maldon and other Old English Poems*, Macmillan, 1965.
8 Riordan, James, 'The Clever Brothers', *Tales from Tartary*, Kestrel.

Chapter 2
1 Holt, *op. cit.*
2 Crossley-Holland, Kevin, *The Wild Man*, Andre Deutsch, 1976.
3 Lane, Harlan, *The Wild Boy of Aveyron*, Allen & Unwin, 1977.
4 Gilson, Etienne, 'Learning as Actualising', *A Gilson Reader*, Doubleday, 1957.

Chapter 3
1 Brecht, Bertolt, *Poems 1913–1956*, Eyre Methuen, 1981.
2 Lawrence, D. H., *Fantasia of the Unconscious*, Penguin.
3 Opie, Iona and Peter, *Children's Games in Street and Playground*, Oxford, 1969.
4 Hopkins, G. M., *Poems and Prose*, Penguin, 1964.
5 Wordsworth, William, *op. cit.*

6   Pinch, A. and Armstrong M., *op. cit.*
7   Buber, Martin, *Between Man and Men*, Fontana, 1974.

Chapter 4
1   Mark, Jan, *Books for Keeps*, March 1984.
2   Pinch, A. and Armstrong M., *op. cit.*
3   Twain, M., *Huckleberry Finn*, Penguin, 1966.
4   Hutchins, Pat, *The Surprise Party*, Puffin.
5   Mark, Jan, 'Send 3/4d. I'm Going to a Dance,' *Nothing to be Afraid of*, Kestrel, 1980.
6   Hadley, Eric, 'Children Writing Stories', *Use of English*, Vol. 35., No. 1, 1983.

Chapter 5
1   Hadley, Eric, 'Children Writing Stories', *op. cit.*
2   Ahlberg, J. and A., *Jeremiah in the Dark Wood*, Fontana Lion, 1980.
3   Dickinson, Peter, *Chance, Luck and Destiny*, Penguin, 1977.
4   Manheim, R., *Grimm's Tales for Young and Old*, Gollancz, 1979.
5   Byars, Betsy, *The Eighteenth Emergency*, Penguin, 1976.
6   Mark, Jan, 'William's Version', *Nothing to be Afraid of*, Kestrel, 1980.
7   Heide, F. P., *The Shrinking of Treehorn*, Penguin, 1975.
8   Sendak, M., *Where the Wild Things Are*, Penguin.
9   Oram, H. and Kitamura M., *Angry Arthur*, Penguin, 1984.
10   Baum, W., *The Expedition*, Blackie, 1976.
11   *Language Performance in Schools*, DES, 1984.
12   Anno, M., *Anno's Journey*, Bodley Head, 1978.

Chapter 6
1   Hutchins, Pat, *Rosie's Walk*, Puffin.
2   Chapman, A. (ed.), *Literature of the American Indians*, New American Library, 1975.
3   See Smith, F., *Essays into Literacy*, Heinemann, 1983.
4   Cook, C., *The Play Way*, Heinemann, 1919.

Chapter 7
1   Lawrence, D. H., *The Rainbow*, Penguin, 1972.
2   Lawrence, D. H., 'Hymns in a Man's Life', *Phoenix 2*, Heinemann, 1968.
3   Baudelaire, Spleen LXXVII, *Les Fleurs du Mal*, Blackwell's French Texts.
4   Blake, W., *Complete Poetry and Prose*, Nonesuch Library, 1967.
5   Quoted in Armstrong, M., *Closely Observed Children*, Writers and Readers, 1980.
6   Evans, G. E., *Ask the Fellows Who Cut the Hay*, Faber, 1969.

7 Darwish, M., Al-Qasim, S., Adonis., *Victims of a Map*, Al Saqi Books, Zed Press, 1984.

8 Darwish, M. et al., *op. cit.*

9 Paynter, J., Voices, Moods and Messages, Sound Machines, Sound Patterns (Vols. 1–4) of *All Kinds of Music*, Oxford, 1976.

10 In Orton, R., (ed.), *Electronic Music for Schools*, CUP, 1981.

11 Paynter, J., *op. cit.*

12 The address for Topic Records is 27 Nassington Road, London, NW3.

13 In Paynter and Mellors, *Resources of Music Series*, CUP, 1973.

14 Gerould, G. H., *The Ballad of Tradition*, Galaxy, 1957.

15 Logue, C., *War Music*, Cape, 1981.

16 Styles, M., *I Like that Stuff*, CUP, 1984.

Chapter 8

1 Benjamin, W., *Illuminations*, Fontana.

2 *Books for Keeps*, Summer 1984.

3 Brecht, Bertolt, *op. cit.*

4 Lawrence, D. H., *The Rainbow*, Penguin, 1972.

5 Tolstoy, L., *Fables and Fairy Tales*, New English Library, 1962.

6 Brecht, Bertold, *Short Stories (1921–1946)*, Methuen.

Chapter 9

1 Shah, I., 'Melon City', *Caravan of Dreams*, Quartet, 1978.

2 Brecht, Bertolt, *Brecht on Theatre*, Eyre Methuen, 1978.

3 Waley, A., *The No Plays of Japan*, Allen & Unwin, 1965.

4 Pinch, A., and Armstrong, M., *op. cit.*

Bibliography

This short listing is a way of acknowledging a debt to writers who have been so influential on my own thinking that no single reference within the text would have been adequate:

Berger, J., *Another Way of Telling*, Writers and Readers, 1982.
Donaldson, M., *Children's Minds*, Fontana, 1978.
Hourd, M., *The Education of the Poetic Spirit*, Heinemann, 1949.
Kohl, H., *The Open Classroom*, Methuen, 1970.
      36 Children, Penguin 1972.
      Reading, How to, Penguin, 1974.
Jones, R. M., *Fantasy and Feeling in Education*, Penguin, 1972.
Smith, F., *Reading*, CUP, 1978.
      Writing and the Writer, Heinemann, 1982.
Trelease, J., *The Read-Aloud Book*, Penguin, 1984.
Zipes, F., *Breaking the Magic Circle*, Heinemann.
Fairy Tale and the Art of Subversion, Heinemann.

I feel I owe a special mention to Geoffrey Summerfield who 'trained' me and the ever-green *Junior Voices* (Books 1 – 4), Penguin, 1970. Also his more recent collection *Poetry World* (1 and 2), Bell and Hyman, 1983. Equally, as far as story collections are concerned, I've found the *Storyhouse* series (Orange, Yellow, Red, Blue and Green) invaluable (eds. Jackson, D., and Pepper, D., Oxford, 1979).

Two recent collections of plays to look out for:
Fitzpatrick, S., *The Gold of Lies* and *Cheating Death*, CUP, 1985.

And finally, for any teacher intent upon stimulating their pupils visually there is David Macaulay's series of books (Collins): *City; Cathedral; Castle; Pyramid; Underground; Mill.*

Teaching Matters

Teaching Poetry in the Secondary School

Veronica O'Brien

Poetry is the area that provides most problems for the English teacher. Children often reach secondary school with little or no experience of poetry and are often hostile to it. *Teaching Poetry in the Secondary School* gives strategies for overcoming that hostility and explores in detail the many ways 'into' poetry. Veronica O'Brien draws on her extensive teaching experience to provide friendly and authoritative advice on a range of common problems, and provides a useful body of poems for use in particular circumstances. The main body of the book provides a wealth of ideas, material and strategies for use with fourth, fifth and sixth year students, with an emphasis on making the poetry lesson an enjoyable and profitable shared experience. The author draws on more than 180 poems, and several detailed discussions are included, as well as an appendix listing the sources of poems mentioned in the text.

Edward Arnold

Teaching Matters

Teaching Shakespeare

Veronica O'Brien

In *Teaching Shakespeare*, Veronica O'Brien provides a variety of imaginative and yet practical strategies through which teachers and pupils are invited to 'meet' Shakespeare, and describes how the classroom experience of the plays may begin in pleasure and end in understanding. She discusses how certain plays can be introduced to pupils early in the secondary school, and gives suggestions for abridgement and explication. Methods of approaching many plays with middle and upper forms, including examination classes, are explored in detail. This book will be particularly helpful to teachers who have taught the plays for many years, but who are looking for some fresh ideas, and to those who are relatively new to English teaching or are non-specialists.

Edward Arnold

Teaching Matters

Approaching Classroom Drama

Rosemary Linnell

In *Approaching Classroom Drama*, Rosemary Linnell provides guidance for both the experienced drama teacher and the non-specialist who are looking for fresh ideas on how to introduce and develop drama in the classroom. Specific advice is given on how to control the development of a lesson, on the types of theme which can best be explored with different age groups, and on planning a sequence of lessons. As well as examining the nature of dramatic activity and discussing drama as a timetabled sub-ject, the author shows how drama can be used to explore aspects of a variety of other school subjects.

Edward Arnold

Teaching Matters

Performance Skills in Drama

Rosemary Linnell

A companion volume to *Approaching Classroom Drama* by the same author, *Performance Skills in Drama* is both a searching analysis of the role of performance in education and an invaluable guide for all those concerned to help young people to communicate their ideas and feelings. This book covers the development of performance skills, the use of texts and improvisation, and gives a detailed step by step description of the planning and staging of a school play. Plenty of practical examples are included throughout the text, and there are also exercises, checklists and suggestions for ways of integrating public performance into a wider learning experience. Without in any way dictating a single approach to 'the school play' or 'examination texts', this book attempts to motivate those concerned with young people's theatre to extend their thinking and to venture into a variety of forms of communication.

Edward Arnold